EQUIPPED TO GO ...

A guide to personal and public evangelism

DAVE SMETHURST

Sovereign World

EQUIPPED TO GO!

Sovereign World Limited
PO Box 777
Tonbridge
Kent TN11 9XT
England

ISBN 1 85240 059 5

Typeset by CRB Typesetting Services, Ely, Cambs.
Printed in England by Richard Clay Ltd, Bungay, Suffolk.

INDEX

CREDITS:
Deep appreciation to:

Mr Neil Lehmann: For typing and re-arranging this manual.
Allan Weatherall: For the graphic work and alterations.
My wife, Margurita and my daughter, Deborah: For proof reading and correcting.

DEDICATION

To my dear wife, Margurita
and my children -Deborah, Paul and Ruth who
have stood with me through the years of
frontline evangelism.
To Pastor and Mrs Earle Davies who trained me
in the foundations of personal and public
evangelism.
But mostly in honour of the
LORD JESUS CHRIST
who promised that if I followed Him, He would
make me a fisher of men.

FOREWORD

We live with all its danger and potential at the edge of the next Millenium. Considered by many Christian leaders the most significant opportunity for evangelism in all of Church history, the final years of the twentieth century have already proved a witness to awesome demonstrations of the power of God to change people's lives all around the world.

In this Decade of Harvest our greatest need in the Church (next only to being a 'people who know their God') is to be both practically and supernaturally equipped to 'do exploits'; specific power and direction to take that Gospel, both publically and personally, from the Jerusalems and Samarias of our own homes and neighbourhoods to the 'ends of the earth'.

Dave Smethurst has given his life to this task, and a significant part of it to help others do it too. In his years of both national and international ministry as an effective instrument in God's hands, he has learned much in how to practically equip others in the challenging and rewarding privilege of leading people to Christ. This seminar outline book is the fruit of those multitude of hours; the essence of what he has longed to impart to others in helping accomplish the great Unfinished Task. Jesus said 'The harvest is great but the labourers are few; pray the Lord of the harvest that He may send forth labourers'. Pray that prayer. Listen to the Lord of the Unreaped Fields. And let these insights from God's Word help 'equip *you* to go'.

Winkie Pratney

YOU CAN BE A PERSUASIVE WITNESS

2 Corinthians 5:14–20 informs every Christian that they have a ministry. God has given us a *ministry of reconciliation* (verse 18) and He's committed to us (verse 19) the *word of reconciliation*. Verse 20 says, we are ambassadors for Christ. We are here in His place representing Him before needy man, urging and begging him to be reconciled to God through Jesus Christ.

If you've ever prayed, 'God, I'm serious about serving You, please use me in your service' God has taken you seriously and that prayer should be followed by action. God has given us our *marching orders*; in Mark 16:15 Jesus instructed us, 'Go into all the world (all your world) and preach the gospel to every person'. Note that this is a command from the Lord Jesus, it is not optional. The challenge is to rouse ourselves from the attitude that winning people to Christ is a week-end hobby in which we might or might not participate. Endeavouring to bring people to Christ is a matter of life and death – eternal life and death. We've got to take it seriously. If God took the salvation of the lost so seriously that He gave heaven's best how dare we take it lightly and give less than our best in winning people to Jesus.

Jesus said in Matthew 10:32, 'If you confess me before men I will confess you before My Father in heaven'. One of the highest forms of gratitude we can show the Lord Jesus is to confess to others how extremely kind and generous He has been to us in dying and rising again to save us.

Jesus wants us all to be His witnesses, as Spirit-filled people we have no excuse. In Acts 1:8 Jesus said 'And you shall receive power when the Holy Spirit has come upon you and you shall be witnesses unto Me'. We do the Holy Spirit a great disservice in not using His power and anointing for the reason intended, that is, to win people to Christ.

Many Christians fear that in being Christ's witness that they will not be able to convince people of their need of Him. A witness in court never has to convince the court regarding a verdict. All the witness has to do is to honestly and clearly share their experience. The court then makes up its mind. Our duty is to honestly and clearly share our experience of Jesus. It's the Holy Spirit's job to convince people of their need of Christ and He does it extremely well.

You are a Winner every time you Witness
When witnessing you are:
(a) *Working with the Holy Spirit*, not Him with you; He is doing most of the work. When we leave a person after sharing Christ with them, the Holy Spirit remains and deals with them. For this reason you are a winner every time you witness. You are working with the one whose power created the universe.

(b) *Sharing the incorruptible seed* according to 1 Peter 1:23.

Isaiah 55:10–11 states that God's Word will never return to Him void and fruitless.

All Jesus asks is that we share our experience of Him and what His blood has done in our lives.

Vital Tips for Being an Effective Soul Winner:

1. Get to know Jesus better

Philippians 3:10 says, 'That I may know Him ...'. The emphasis there is an intimate knowing in a personal relationship – so personal, that between husbands and wives, that relationship produces children. We need to get to know Jesus so intimately that our relationship with Him, in a spiritual sense, produces children for the Kingdom of God. When people look at us they should see that we are so in love with Jesus and He with us, and that relationship radiates from our lives. It should make them want to know Him. We get to know Jesus better daily through the Word of God as we read and obey it, daily prayer, praise and worship as we open our hearts to Him.

2. Follow Jesus

In Matthew 4:19 Jesus said, 'Follow me and I will make you fishers of men'.
1 Peter 2:21 says, 'Christ has left us an example for us to follow in His steps'. We find the footsteps of Jesus daily in the Word of God. It is then up to us to put our feet into His footprints, imitate Him and obey His Word. It stands to reason that the closer we follow Him the more people we will catch.

3. Uplift Jesus

In John 12:32 Jesus said, 'If I am uplifted I will draw all men unto myself'. Jesus is the magnetic drawing power of the gospel. We must be sure when sharing our personal testimonies and talking about our experience that we uplift Jesus. He is the One who has saved us and made us children of God. Uplift Jesus with your life, your actions and with your words and people will be drawn to Him.

4. Be Persuasive

In 2 Corinthians 5:20 the apostle Paul says, 'We beg you, as Christ's ambassadors, be reconciled to God'. Now that's persuasive witnessing. There are so many people who know a lot of facts of the Gospel but just don't know the simple decision they need to make to commit their lives to Jesus Christ.

What we need to do is lovingly urge them into that life changing decision. We can't make it for them, but knowing the 'terror of the Lord we persuade men' that they need to receive Christ. Being abrasive, dogmatic and forceful will never win anyone to Christ. Yes, we need to be persuasive but we are not out to win arguments, we are out to win people; we are out to love them into a relationship with Jesus. 1 Peter 3:15 says, 'Be always ready to give an answer to anyone who asks you a reason of the hope that is in you, with gentleness and respect'. When we witness to someone they should feel bigger not smaller, respected not degraded and cut down. They should want the relationship with Jesus that we are offering and they will come to that acceptance by the gracious way we deal with them.

When sharing the Gospel, or sharing our testimony of Christ remember to bring the seeking soul to a decision. The preaching of the Gospel is incomplete without urging them to a commitment. 'What will you do with Christ now that you know about Him?' This is the vital question. Be gentle but be persuasive. Most people are lazy and will put off decisions, especially those that have far-reaching consequences. We need to urge them to decide for Christ and show them how to receive Him into their lives.

The devil is pushing people into sin, sinful lives and hell quicker than we realise. How much more shouldn't we be one jump ahead of him in urging people to come to Christ.

If they were drowning in a river unable to swim and you were standing on the river bank with a lifeline would they need to debate whether they needed you to rescue them or not. They would be screaming at you for help. They are drowning/perishing in their sins. You are throwing them a lifeline in Jesus Christ. Do they need to debate whether they should receive Him or not. Of course not! Jesus says we are to go and make disciples of all nations, Matthew 28:19. Luke 14:23 Jesus uses the parable urging us to 'go into the highways and byways and compel people to come in' to His Kingdom.

There are so many who know the facts of the Gospel but are standing on the brink of making the right decision for Christ. With our help and sincere urging they will make that decision correctly.

Please refer to the method, 'How to Lead a Soul to Jesus Christ'. (See Page 96) Use this little method if you don't have one of your own to bring people to Jesus. Look up the verses of Scripture, underline them, get to know where they are in your Bible and memorise them.

Paste the method in the front of your Bible and don't be scared to refer to it when leading someone to Jesus. They won't know what you're looking at and besides that, you are working with God and therefore are in command of the situation. Having taken them through the various steps to the prayer of commitment, lead them in that prayer audibly wherein they invite Jesus to be the Lord and Saviour of their lives.

Whatever you do, don't leave them at that point. Give them the assurance of their salvation from the Word of God, not from their feelings.

Then give them the guidelines on how to begin growing in Christ. It is important as a babe in Christ that they grow to maturity to bear fruit and eventually bring others to Christ. (Refer to the notes on *'Counsellors Instructions'*, *'Who you are in Christ'* and *'Follow Up of a New Christian'* for the basics of a follow up programme with the person you have led to Jesus Christ.) The basis of effective follow up is being a friend to them in Christ.

See Page 96 for *'How to Lead a Soul to Christ'* Bible Insert

YOU CAN LEAD A SOUL TO JESUS CHRIST!

Proverbs 11:30 'He who wins souls is wise'. Daniel 12:3 'Those who are wise, the people of God shall shine as brightly as the sun's brilliance, and those who turn many from sin to righteousness will glitter like the stars for ever'. So if we would be wise before God and man, and if we would be 'God's stars' shining brightly in this dark world, let us bring people from sin to righteousness by leading them to Jesus Christ.

Two Reasons why People aren't Soul Winners

Firstly, they say they lack boldness and courage.

In Acts 1:8 the Lord Jesus said we would receive power when the Holy Spirit came upon us and we would be His witnesses. Jesus Christ is the One who will baptise us with the Holy Spirit and fire. Ask Him right now to fill you with the Holy Spirit, or re-fill you if you've 'run dry'. He will 'drench' you with the Holy Spirit and His anointing for this service, so that you will overflow with a loving and confident witness.

Just in case you're saying 'I'm too shy; I couldn't bring someone to a decision for Christ', let Andrew's example in Scripture encourage you. Every time Andrew is mentioned in the Bible he's bringing people to Jesus. In John 1 Simon Peter, in John 6, a boy with his lunch, and in John 12 some Greeks.

The second reason people don't win others to Christ is because they don't know how to.

I'd like to teach you how with the following method:

1.   Engage in Conversation

We have a message to share and we can't do it effectively without talking. Watch how the Holy Spirit will steer the conversation and give you a point of contact, or an opening to talk about spiritual matters. Ask the person if you may share a personal experience and then share very clearly YOUR PERSONAL TESTIMONY OF JESUS CHRIST.

2.   Ask where they Stand in Relation to Jesus Christ

Simply ask 'Have you received Jesus Christ as your Lord and Saviour?' This gently puts them 'on the spot' and confronts them with their need. You can ask them:

(a) 'Are you saved?' But then explain what God wants to save them **from**: sin and its awful consequences – fruitlessness and misery in life and being separated forever from God for eternity. And saved to enjoy adventure and fruitfulness in Christ now and eternity with Him in heaven.

(b) 'Are you born-again?' Explain from John 3 what that means in terms of their spirit being 'dead' and cut off from God by a barrier of sin, needing to be cleansed by the blood of Jesus, and revived into a relationship with God. If you ask:

(c) 'Are you a Christian?' You must explain that a true Christian is a 'Christ-one'; having Jesus Christ really and truly living in them.

(d) When dealing with devoutly religious people I don't waste time asking the above questions (they believe they are saved and are Christians by belonging to their church and having gone through the sacraments.) I ask them purposely 'Have you made Jesus Christ Lord of your life?' The word 'Lord' means MASTER or BOSS. You'll then find out very quickly if they have a right relationship with the Lord Jesus Christ. Acts 2:36 says 'God has made this Jesus whom you crucified both Lord and Christ'. He is both Saviour and Lord, and we must yield to Him as such.

(e) You can ask very pointedly 'If you died today, are you sure you'd go to Heaven?' If they truly know Christ they'll be sure of that.

(f) For the more obstinate, who insist they don't need Jesus as their Saviour, you can ask 'Arriving at the gates of Heaven, what reason would you give for being allowed in?' Any other reason than 'I've received Jesus Christ as my Lord and Saviour, and I'll be allowed in by the merits of His blood is unacceptable to God'. No 'good works' (Titus 3:5), no mediation of the 'saints' (1 Timothy 2:5), nor church membership can gain us access into Heaven. In John 14:6 Jesus said He is the ONLY WAY to the Father and Hebrews 9:12 states that we are redeemed eternally only by His blood.

3. Why must they Receive Jesus?

Simply because the Bible says they are sinners. (Romans 3:23; 1 John 1:8) Every one of us has broken God's moral laws (the commandments). We've missed the mark and fallen short of God's glorious purposes for us, like an archer whose arrows have all fallen short of the target.

4. The Results of Sin

Unless people realise the danger they're in, they don't know they need to be rescued. All of us are sinners because we have a sinful nature that causes us to sin. We are not called sinners because we commit individual sins, but because of the sinful nature we have. This sinful condition has rendered us, in God's eyes:

LOST (Luke 19:10)
GUILTY BEFORE GOD
(Romans 3:19)
CONDEMNED (John 3:18, 36)
SPIRITUALLY DEAD
(Ephesians 2:1)
SEPARATED FROM GOD
(Isaiah 59:2)
That's terrible!

5. If their Sin is not Removed

(a) Their life will be fruitless. All the beautiful priorities God wants to give them will never be theirs; i.e. Peace, Joy, Purpose, Fulfilment and the quality of Eternal Life (Ephesians 2:1–10).

(b) They will be separated from God's presence forever in eternity (Romans 3:23; Revelation 14:11).

6. Only God, by the Blood of Jesus, can Cleanse and Redeem them

This is the 'Good News' of the Gospel. Please tell people that the Blood of Jesus Christ:

(a) REDEEMS us back to God from satan's kingdom (Ephesians 1:7; Colossians 1:13, 14).

(b) CLEANSES us from all sin (1 John 1:7–9)

(c) JUSTIFIES us – makes us righteous before God, just as if we'd never sinned (Romans 5:9; 2 Corinthians 5:21) and accepted by God (Ephesians 1:6).

Matthew 4:19 Jesus said 'Follow me and I will make you fishers of men'. This command is also an encouragement that Jesus Himself will make us fishers of men – if we follow Him. A personal commitment to follow Jesus closely is the first essential in being a fisher of men.

(d) SANCTIFIES us – sets us apart for God and His exciting purposes (Hebrews 13:12) and draws us close to God (Ephesians 2:13); no longer separated.

7. What should they do now?

REPENT – which means change their minds:

(a) about God – He loves them and does not want them to perish in their sins; and

(b) about themselves – that they're lost and on their way to hell (John 3:16; Acts 17:30; Matthew 9:13; Luke 13:3, 5).

BELIEVE ON THE LORD JESUS CHRIST – which means to believe that He died for them, shedding His blood to forgive them, and rose again from the dead to give them eternal life (Acts 17:30; 1 John 5:11–13).

RECEIVE JESUS AS SAVIOUR AND LORD – in prayer express the commitment to believe on Him and invite Him into their life (Romans 10:9, 10, 13).

The Prayer of Commitment

There is an art in giving an altar call, whether it's done publicly or personally. Even when a large crowd responds after a Gospel message you're still leading individuals to Jesus Christ. Please be gentle while you're being persuasive. Remember the person you're dealing with has had so many amazing facts delivered to them during the time you've shared and their minds are probably boggling with the shock of realising their desperate need of Christ. Don't push them. Rather encourage them by saying 'Now that you know the great need to have your sins forgiven by receiving Christ, I'd like to pray for you. Would you mind?' Once you have their consent say to them 'I'd like you to identify with my prayer ... would you pray with me?'. You haven't charged in, you've led them gently into the prayer. Most people will not know what to pray and will be glad you offered to lead them.

If your 'enquirer' is reluctant to pray with you:

(a) It could be out of embarrassment.

If there are others in close proximity ask them to leave or the two of you move to a private place.

(b) If they 'fear' the unknown that they are letting themselves into, simply encourage them that they have nothing to fear; they're not going to become weird at all. After all, they know you and you're pretty normal ... aren't you?

(c) They want some time to think it over.

Ask the Holy Spirit what you should do. If you sense a red 'stop light', back off and say you'll call them the next day. Whatever you do, don't let them 'off the hook'. The devil is fighting his hardest to keep them from getting saved.

If I don't sense a 'red light' I press them gently but firmly to a decision with the following illustration:

'If you were drowning in a nearby lake and I had a life line to pull you out, would you need to think or debate whether you should catch it or not? No, you'd be screaming at me to rescue you. Now, in a far more serious way, you are "drowning" in your sins. It is certain you will perish if you're not rescued. Would you now like to pray with me receiving Christ as your Rescuer?'

You will find most will respond to that challenge, but remember to be gentle, don't crush them!

(d) You may find someone saying this 'I wish I could believe in Christ but I can't. There's something stopping me.' You know who that is! Just say to the person that you're going to pray over them right on the spot and they mustn't be surprised at the way you pray. Don't alarm them but let them know that the devil is blocking them from coming to Christ and putting fear into them. Don't shout, but pray firmly like this 'In the name of Jesus, I rebuke you, you deceiving devil. Take your evil influence and go from this person now'. Now ask the person if they will pray with you. You'll be amazed how many in the past have simply relaxed and said to me 'Yes, I'm ready now'.

A Simple Prayer
Ask them to repeat this prayer aloud after you and direct the words to God Himself, meaning them with all their heart.

'Dear God, I come to you as a sinner, knowing I need your forgiveness and that I can't save myself. I thank you for loving me so much that you sent your Son, Jesus, to die for me. Lord Jesus Christ, I believe you rose again from the dead and are alive to save me now. I receive you as my Saviour and make you Lord of my life. I repent of my sin and I'm sorry that I've neglected you in the past. But that stops right now. Please forgive all my sin and give me your gift of life. Thank you for hearing my prayer. From now on, I'll do my best to follow and serve you.'

Assurance of Salvation
Don't let this precious new Christian leave your company without giving them the assurance of their salvation. They need to *know* that whether they felt any emotion or not, in praying that prayer GOD'S WORD SAYS they are saved and have God's gift of eternal life. Take them to these verses of scripture and let them read them aloud for themselves, being assured that because God has said it, it has happened!

(a) Their sin is forgiven and cleansed by the blood of Jesus (Ephesians 1:7).

(b) They've been redeemed (bought back to God) from sin and it's awful consequences (Hebrews 9:12, 22).

(c) They've been given God's gift of eternal life (John 6:47; Romans 6:23b).

(d) Jesus has received them (John 6:37) and made them a child of God (John 1:12).

The WORD OF GOD is their proof of all this (1 John 5:11–13).

Before they leave your company, urge them to 'get out of the starting blocks and into the race' by beginning to serve Jesus each day and *read God's Word* starting at John's Gospel; *talk with God* each day in prayer; *rely daily on the indwelling presence of the Holy Spirit* to help and strengthen them; *fellowship with other believers* – get them to church with you and into a home fellowship group (if it's good enough for you it's good enough for them) and urge them to *share with others around them* about their new relationship with Jesus.

HOW TO BE AN EXPERT
FISHERMAN
The Courtesy & Etiquette of Witnessing

Matthew 4:19 Jesus said 'Follow me and I will make you fishers of men'. This command is also an encouragement that Jesus Himself will make us fishers of men – if we follow Him. A personal commitment to follow Jesus closely is the first essential in being a fisher of men.

5 Points that Distinguish an Expert Fisherman:
1. His Purpose is Clear
We must not be distracted from our task of personal evangelism by relatives or friends. Luke 14:26 Jesus said 'If anyone comes to Me and does not hate (love Me far above) his father, mother wife, children, brothers, sisters, even his own life, he cannot be My disciple'. He must come first and His claims on our lives must be responded to before any of the others.

We must not be side-tracked by ambitions or promotions in a career situation that would distract us from our purpose. In Matthew 6:33 Jesus said we are to seek first the Kingdom of God. This means to be implicitly obedient to the King of the Kingdom, seek His interests before our own.

2. His Preparation is Careful
We must be prepared in prayer each day, as well as in personal holiness. Our lives are a great weapon to win people to Christ. They win us the right to speak and earn us those precious opportunities to influence folk to Christ.

Pointers to help you in your preparation:
(a) It is essential to have an unhurried time each day for prayer and Bible reading. The best time is at the start of each day. (Isaiah 50:4, 5)

(b) Live as a true child of God, not as a weird fanatic. Be genuine, don't be a phony. Be real and be joyful. Be yourself, and let Jesus be Himself in you. In Matthew 5:13–16 Jesus says that we are a lamp to guide those close to us to Christ. We are a 'city set on a hill' to guide those from afar to Him. We are to 'let our light shine before men'.

Jesus said we are salt. Salt makes people thirsty. If we were saltier the world would be thirstier for Christ.

(c) Don't condemn people for their way of life. You'll never win them that way. There is enough condemnation in the world already. If you want to win them and change their life-style, bring them to Jesus Christ. You don't approve of their sinful activities but offer them Jesus. He's the One who will change them. Jesus was called in Matthew 11:19 'the friend of despised tax-gatherers and sinners'. John 3:17 says He came 'not into the world to condemn the world, but that the world through Him might be saved'.

(d) Have a heart of love. Don't be argumentative, dogmatic or forceful. That may win arguments but doesn't win people. Be a considerate friend to those around you. I believe our love for the lost is spelt T.I.M.E. – time spent with them letting the love of God flow through us to touch their hearts. Romans 5:5 says that the love of God has already been shed abroad in our hearts by the Holy Spirit.

3.   His Place is Chosen

A fisherman fishes where the fish are. We can't separate ourselves with a 'holier than thou' attitude from sinners who need Christ. We rub shoulders with them every day and that's the place to fish. In fact the Holy Spirit will guide us to create our own opportunities where there don't seem to be any. In 2 Timothy 4:2 the apostle Paul urges us to preach the word and be ready in season (when we have an opportunity) and out of season (when we don't have an opportunity).

4.   His Person is Concealed

We mustn't be a stumbling block to that needy person through selfish living or blatant sin. Philippians 2:14 says 'Do everything without complaining or arguing so that you may become blameless and pure, children of God without fault in a crooked and depraved generation in which you shine like stars in the universe'. I know when sharing our testimony we use the words *I, me, my, myself,* however our motive, in terms of John 12:32 must be to uplift Jesus. His command to us in Acts 1:8 is that we be witnesses unto Him. The cry of the world is expressed in John 12:21 'Sirs we would see Jesus'. Our response in terms of 1 John 1:2 & 3 should be ' . . . we show unto you that eternal life . . . that which we have seen and heard declare we unto you . . . '

5.   Sharing your Testimony

Tell it simply and without theological cliches that the unsaved don't understand. Be natural, remember you're sharing what your relationship with Jesus has done for you. You're not entering into a theological debate. As you share your testimony, use the Scripture. Memorise a few vital verses to impart into their lives, such as Romans 3:23, 1 John 1:7, John 1:12, John 6:37, John 6:47, Revelation 3:20. 2 Timothy 3:15 says 'The Scriptures are able to make thee wise unto salvation'. It is the Word of God that quickens and makes alive, but our testimony warms and inspires.

It is the link between the Word of God and the reality of salvation in that person's life.

6.   His Patience is Constant

An expert fisherman waits patiently for a bite; he doesn't quit. We are to witness patiently, pray long and never give up in endeavouring to bring needy souls to Christ. Let me urge you to pray for those you are concerned about winning to Christ.

You're praying according to God's will. 2 Peter 3:9 tells us God is not willing that any should perish and 1 Timothy 2:4 states that God wants all men to be saved. Go for it with all your being.

Intercession means intense prayer and pleading with God on behalf of those who don't have anyone else to pray for them, especially for those who don't know Christ. Start by praying for those you know, for:

- The Lord to convict them of their need of Christ.
- The Holy Spirit to work in their hearts to draw them to Christ.
- That they may see Christ in you.
- For opportunities to witness to them.
- For wisdom to use opportunities well.
- For the right attitude and the right words at the right time.

Intercession is the power behind fruitful evangelism. Your evangelistic endeavour is won in the area of prayer and intercession beforehand. A soul-winner or fisher of men is an intercessor in action. After you've prayed and interceded, the next step is to go out and reach for Christ. First of all you contact God on their behalf, and then you contact them on God's behalf by going to them with the Word of Life.

Here's how you do it:

Ephesians 3:20 'God is able to do exceedingly abundantly above all that we ask or imagine, according to His power that works in us'.

If God is able to do exceedingly abundantly, then how dare we think small when we enter into this tremendous partnership of prayer with the Creator of the Universe.

Think big! Imagine great things happening when you pray. Picture in your mind the end result of what you anticipate should happen, such as your friend or family member being committed to Jesus, serving the Lord effectively, in church with you, on their feet with their hands raised, worshipping Jesus as Lord of their lives. Picture it like that and *aim your prayers and faith at that target*.

But remember to 'take the lid off your faith' and say to God 'do it like that Lord only better, because you are able to do exceedingly, abundantly, above all that I ask or imagine'.

From individuals you will then pray for families. For those who live on your street, for your suburb, for your town, for your city, for your country, for the whole world.

Imagine 'seeing' the whole suburb around you committed to Jesus, serving Him with all their hearts. When you see them in the street, *see them as potential Christians, and share Christ with them joyfully*.

Desperate Need for Labourers

Matthew 9:36–38 Jesus said 'The harvest is plentiful but the labourers are few. Pray therefore to the Lord of the harvest that he would thrust forth labourers into His harvest'. Can I urge you to pray this prayer right now to the Lord of the harvest?

Dear Heavenly Father, Lord of the harvest, I see that the harvest is plentiful but the labourers are so few. Please thrust forth labourers into your harvest to reap people into your Kingdom. **Here am I Lord, send me!'**

WINNING AND MAKING DISCIPLES

Matthew 28:19–20 *'Go therefore and make disciples of all nations, baptising them ... and teaching them to observe all that I commanded you.'*

2 Timothy 2:2 *'And the things which you have heard from me in the presence of many witnesses these entrust to faithful men (and women) who will be able to teach others also.'*

Faithful People/Disciples ... should have:
1. A hunger for God's Word
2. A thirst for holy living
3. A desire for greater knowledge of God
4. A commitment to the Lordship of Jesus – wanting His will in every matter
5. A desire to be used of God
6. A love for all people

These may not be fully developed, but there should at least be an indication of thse characteristics.

> 1 Thessalonians 2:7 & 8 *'But we prove to be gentle among you, as a nursing mother tenderly cares for her own children, having thus a fond affection for you, we were well pleased to impart to you not only the Gospel of God, but **also our own lives** because you had become very dear to us.'*

We are not called only to reach, but to train by example, i.e. being on time; stopping bad habits; giving of time, talents, resources to expand God's Kingdom to these attitudes and actions will be transmitted to others.

Our Father seeks His children to worship Him in Spirit and in Truth
God does not only want people to be saved and become disciples of His Son, He wants people to worship Him. This is the purpose for which He created us and the reason He went to so much trouble to redeem us back to Himself, through Christ. All of life becomes a worship of our Father, our lives, our actions and our words.

The Vine and the Branches
We are branches in the vine – Jesus Christ. The purpose of a branch is to bear fruit. A branch never strains to bear fruit, but it simply abides in the vine. The vine causes life-giving sap to flow through it and it bears fruit. By abiding in Christ, staying close to Him and not running off and doing our own thing, He causes the life-giving sap of the Holy Spirit to flow through us and thus we bear fruit.

The Prime Fruit God wants from us is Thanksgiving, Praise and Worship

Thanksgiving: Thanksgiving in the Scripture is always related to Salvation. Thank Him for various aspects of the great salvation He has given you.

Praise: This means showing our gratitude for the wonderful things God does for us every day, because we are His children.

Worship: This is glorifying Him for who He is. Everything He does for us flows from who He is. His character and nature is revealed in the many names by which He makes Himself known to us through the Scriptures, such as:

Psalm 91:1 & 2
'The Most High God' – El Elyon (Hebrew) The Ruler and Possessor of Heaven and Earth; the One who is in charge.

'The Almighty' – El Shaddai. The almighty, all-powerful one, constantly pouring out nourishment to His children and meeting their needs.

'Lord' – Jehovah. The One who always is the constant 'I am' – the total provision through Jesus Christ into every need we will ever have.

Jehovah Shammah – He is constantly present with us.

Jehovah Shalom – The Lord is our peace.

Jehovah Jireh – The Lord will provide for us.

Jehovah Nissi – The Lord who gives us constant victory.

Jehovah Tsidkenu – The Lord who clothes us with His Righteousness.

Jehovah Rophe – The Lord who heals us.

Jehovah Ro-hi – The Lord who is our loving, guiding shepherd.

'GOD' – Elohim (Hebrew) – this shows a plurality in one God. Genesis 1:26 'Then God said, "Let us make man in our image" ...'. This denotes two or more in one. The Bible goes on to reveal the tri-une God of Father, Son and Holy Spirit in one Godhead. They made a covenant within themselves that could never be broken, to create, love, redeem man and provide for him. No wonder Moses in Psalm 91:1 and 2 says, 'He that dwelleth in the secret place of the Most High, shall abide under the shadow of the Almighty. I will say of the Lord, He is my refuge and my fortress, my God in Him will I trust'.

WORSHIP GOD FOR WHO HE IS AND HIS SON JESUS CHRIST, WHOM HE SENT, AND THANK THE HOLY SPIRIT FOR BRINGING YOU INTO THIS ETERNAL RELATIONSHIP WITH GOD THROUGH JESUS CHRIST.

You are a branch in order to bear fruit

A branch never strains to bear fruit, it simply abides and bears fruit. Who enjoys the fruit? – I've never seen a branch eating its own fruit. Of course, our Heavenly Gardener enjoys the fruit and then to whomsoever He distributes the fruit. *Your evangelism will flow from your ministry of worship to God your Father and the Lord Jesus Christ.* He will distribute the gracious fruit of the Spirit from your life to others around you: 'love, joy, peace, patience, kindness, goodness, faithfulness, gentleness, self control' (Galatians 5:22–23). *This fruit received by others, will overwhelm them and draw them to Christ.* This is the basis for powerful, effective evangelism and will win you the right to talk to people about Christ.

Spend time worshipping God in your daily devotions ...

... then go right into the day and be led by the Holy Spirit into situations where you can share Christ. You'll find Him leading you into the most amazing conversations. His confidence will well up within you; His love will overflow from you and you'll simply be loving people into a relationship with Jesus.

THREE WORDS ... *GO FOR IT!*

THE SOLUTION TO MAN'S NEED

The Problem

Through disobedience man lost out with God. He gave his allegiance to the devil. God originally gave man rule and dominion over the earth. Man gave it to satan and he became the god of this world. He is causing disasters and devastation on the earth – Genesis 3:13–24.

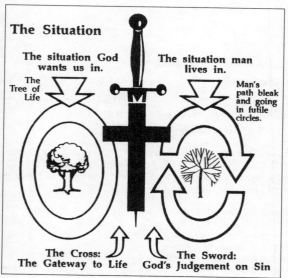

The Situation

The situation God wants us in.

The Tree of Life

The situation man lives in.

Man's path bleak and going in futile circles.

The Cross: The Gateway to Life

The Sword: God's Judgement on Sin

God's Curse:

Because of man's disobedience, sin separated him from God, his source of pure joy, fulfilment, purpose and eternal life.

Problems of the Curse:

1. Man lost his relationship and fellowship with God and lost his dominion of the earth to satan.
2. A breakdown of relationship between man and wife
– Genesis 3:16.
3. Man would have to work all his life straining for minimum results
– Genesis 3:17–19.

The Remedy

A relationship with God through Jesus Christ provides the potential for:

1. Man to live in fellowship with God, enjoying His presence and blessing and in Christ to regain his dominion over satan.

2. Husbands to love their wives and wives to submit to loving husbands – unity in the marriage.

3. Under Jesus' authority to rebuke and renounce the effects of the curse, for profitable living.

The Way Out

1. Man must realise he is trapped in his futility.
2. He must want help.
3. He must repent of his selfish efforts and own works.
4. He must turn to Jesus who was 'hung on a tree' and became a curse for us.
5. Receive Jesus as Lord and Saviour.

The Sinner's Prayer:

This must embody:

1. Being aware that they are a sinner (Romans 3:23).
2. Jesus died for their sin (Romans 5:6 & 8).
3. They must repent of their sin and turn from it (Acts 3:19).
4. Ask His forgiveness and cleansing in the blood of Christ (1 John 1:7–9).
5. Yield to Him as Lord and Saviour (Romans 10:9, 10 & 13).

The Blood of Jesus – Effective on our Behalf

In the Old Testament, a lamb's blood was sprinkled seven times in the Holy of Holies. In Hebrews 9:12 & 24 Jesus' blood presented before the Father in Heaven was shed from seven areas of His body:

> From His head – *to guard our minds and heal our thoughts.*
> From His back – *for the burden of life to be lifted.*
> From His two hands – *to guard what our hands will do.*
> From His two feet – *to guard where our feet will go.*
> From His side – *to guard our heart and our will.*

Now we have Salvation

Therefore we can go to the Tree of Life from which Adam and Eve were forbidden. We don't have to live under the curse and struggles of life any longer.

What is the Tree of Life?

It is the Life of Jesus. He wants to be our total supply, spiritually, mentally, socially and physically. Once we had to struggle for these things under satan's rule, now Jesus says, 'I will supply these things abundantly'.

We are to advertise to the world that Jesus is our Provision and Provider

John 17:10. Jesus prayed: 'I am glorified in them' – our advertisement of the 'Tree of Life' providing for us in every way. Jesus wants to be our total supply. Bring it all to Him!

Now we are called upon to do the Works of Jesus:

The Holy Spirit in us gives us His power to live and do as Jesus did – John 14:12. We are to:

1. **Preach** – reach out to the lost.

2. **Teach** – to edify the Body.

3. **Heal the sick** – show God's compassion for the needy.

4. **Cast out demons** – deliver others from the dominion of satan.

5. **Live to fulfil the will of the Father.**

6. **Live under the anointing and power of the Holy Spirit.**

7. **Give our lives for others** – put aside the things that would hinder our witness to others so that they may see Christ in us and come to know Him as well.

Final Comment:

Our first calling is to worship God – Philippians 3:3. This we are to do with our lives, actions and words, saying 'Jesus you are my life, my total supply', and live that out in every day life. It glorifies God to live that way.

VICTORY THROUGH THE BLOOD OF JESUS

Revelation 12:11 *'And they overcame the devil by the blood of the Lamb, and by the word of their testimony and they loved not their lives even unto death.'* The power lies in our testimony, our spoken word concerning the blood of Jesus.

What the Word of God teaches us about the Blood of Jesus

1.   The Blood of Jesus has redeemed us, ransomed or bought us back from the devil

Ephesians 1:7 *'In Him we have redemption through His Blood, the forgiveness of our sins according to the riches of His grace which He lavished on us.'*

Hebrews 9:12 *'Neither by the blood of goats and calves, but by His own blood Christ ... obtained eternal redemption for us.'*

2.   The blood of Jesus cleanses us from all sin

1 John 1:7–9 *'But if we walk in the light as He Himself is in the light, we have fellowship one with another, and the blood of Jesus Christ, His Son, cleanses us from all sin ... If we confess our sins He is faithful and just (righteous) to forgive us our sins and to cleanse us from all unrighteousness.'*

The blood keeps on cleansing us, it never stops, as we walk in the light of Jesus' presence and stay in fellowship with one another.

3.   We are justified – made righteous by the blood of Jesus, just as if we had never sinned

Romans 5:9 *'Much more then having now been justified by His blood we shall be saved from the wrath of God through Him.'*

2 Corinthians 5:21 *'He made Him who knew no sin, to be sin on our behalf, that we might become the righteousness of God in Him.'*

God sees us through the blood of Jesus, pure and spotless. He sees us clothed with the righteousness of Jesus, not our own works; therefore we have boldness and confidence to come before His throne of grace to find mercy and help in our time of need – Hebrews 4:14–16. We have confidence to enter God's presence in prayer, through the blood of Jesus Christ.

Hebrews 10:19–20 *'We have confidence to enter the Holy Place by the blood of Jesus by a new and living way which He inaugurated for us through the veil that is His flesh.'*

4.   Through the blood of Jesus we are sanctified – made holy – set apart for God's service

Hebrews 13:12 *'Therefore Jesus also, that He might sanctify the people through His own blood, suffered outside the gate.'*

5. Our conscience is cleansed of all guilt by the blood of Jesus

Hebrews 9:14 *'How much more will the blood of Christ, who through the eternal Spirit offered Himself without blemish to God, cleanse your conscience from dead works to serve the living God.'*

Therefore, in terms of 2 Timothy 1:7

'God has not given us a spirit of fear (caused by guilt of sin), *but of power and love and a sound, disciplined mind.'*

Therefore our testimony/confession of faith regarding the blood of Jesus is as follows:

1. Through the blood of Jesus Christ I have redemption. I am redeemed out of the hand and power of the devil.

2. Through the blood of Jesus all my sins are forgiven. As I walk in the light with Jesus, His blood is continually cleansing me from all sins.

3. Through the blood of Jesus I am justified, made righteous, just as if I had never sinned. I am clothed with His righteousness.

4. Through the blood of Jesus I have access into the presence of God at any time to obtain mercy and help, especially in time of need.

5. Through the blood of Jesus I am sanctified – made holy and set apart for God.

6. Through the blood of Jesus my conscience is cleansed of all guilt and I am free in body, mind, soul and spirit to serve the Lord Jesus Christ.

7. Therefore I have the victory over the devil and I overcome him by the blood of the Lamb and the word of my testimony concerning His blood and I love not my life even unto death.

HOW THE BLOOD OF JESUS AFFECTS OUR DAILY LIVES

Victory over Rebellion

In the garden of Gethsemane Jesus prayed His 'High Priestly' prayer:

> 'Not my will but Thine be done.' (Luke 22:42)

The strain of death was so great upon Him that blood vessels broke in His face, mixed with perspiration and fell to the ground in great drops. That blood shed in the garden speaks of a particular redemption i.e. REDEMPTION FROM REBELLION – exercising our will against the will of God – doing our own thing, and all its awful consequences. From Adam, the human race has insisted on doing its own will and trampling on the will of God. At times people have tried to keep His will in their own power according to the law, but *had no power*, therefore man's fallen rebellious nature could not be yielded to the Father. When Jesus prayed that High Priestly prayer, 'Not My will but Thine be done', He prayed it in our place, as a priest does, representing the people before God. In praying that prayer He shed His blood to redeem our wills so that we too can say, 'Not my will but Thine be done'.

Therefore whenever we struggle in our hearts to obey God, we should picture that blood coming from Jesus' face. It says that our will has been submitted to the will of the Father *in Christ*. Our will has been redeemed and we can claim it by the power of the blood of Jesus. We will then experience the power of the Holy Spirit releasing us to do God's will.

A Prayer ... *'Lord, your blood was shed in the Garden for me. I claim the power of your blood in my life. Holy Spirit release your power now through the blood of Jesus Christ, enabling me to yield my will to the will of the Father. I thank you and claim your peace, victory and power in my life according to the will of God. **Amen.**'*

Jesus shed His blood through the crown of thorns

The thorn was a symbol of God's curse on sin. (Genesis 3:18)

It was fitting for Jesus when suffering on the cross for our redemption from the curse of sin to wear on His brow the symbol of the curse, i.e. the thorn. (Matthew 27:29).

He thus indicated He was taking the curse upon Himself. He shed His blood being pierced by those thorns. That blood speaks of redemption from the curse of sin. So many are living under the curse of sin in the thorns of life. Thorns of hatred, doubt, fear and self-pity, pride, resentment, bitterness ... Only by the power of the blood of Jesus applied by the Holy Spirit are we set free from that curse. We can call on Him praying: 'Holy Spirit, I claim the power of the blood of Jesus shed through the crown of thorns to deliver me from the thorns of this life, the curse of sin, from hatred, doubt, fear, pride, resentment, etc. Amen.'

The blood from His Scourge Wounds

The blood of Jesus was shed from His back and His body as a result of the *scourging or whipping*. Jesus' body was a bleeding pulp. His arteries were slashed open and blood poured out. This shedding of blood says: 'By his stripes we are healed.' (Isaiah 53:5). It speaks of total healing for spirit, soul, mind, body, our homes, our attitudes and relationships. 'Surely He bore our griefs (infirmities) and carried our sorrows (sicknesses).' (Isaiah 53:4).

Sickness and disease are a result of the curse of sin in this world's system, but His blood was shed from those stripes to redeem us from the curse of sin. Therefore a prayer to pray –

> *'Dear God, I claim the redeeming power of Christ's blood to deliver me from sickness, disease, weakness, pain, infirmity and by the stripes of Jesus I receive healing for spirit, soul, mind, body etc. and I thank You for honouring your Word. Amen.'*

Jesus' blood was shed on the cross at Calvary

Nails were driven into His hands and feet and a soldier pierced His side, and forthwith there gushed out blood and water. Jesus cried out 'It is finished'.

His blood shed there was, and is, sufficient and powerful enough to save us and redeem us eternally from sin and God's judgement on sin. When we receive Jesus and believe into what He has done, we are saved, sanctified and set aside for God by the blood of Jesus. (Hebrews 13:12).

All our sins are forgiven, past, present and future. Of course if we continue to sin and thus live rebellious lives, we will reap the consequences on this earth and experience God's chastisement. We will also receive no rewards in heaven. (1 Corinthians 3:11–15)

Therefore we are saved and kept secure by the blood of Jesus. This is total grace. (Ephesians 2:8–9)

'There is now therefore no condemnation to those who are in Christ Jesus.' (Romans 8:1)

'For God did not send His Son into the world to condemn the world but that the world through Him should be saved.' (John 3:17)

PRAISE GOD FOR THE BLOOD OF JESUS CHRIST!

PERSONAL PREPARATION FOR WITNESSING & COUNSELLING

(Spend an unhurried time in prayer with the Lord praying through this 'check list'. Soon it will become part of your life as an ambassador of Jesus Christ.)

1. **James 4:7** 'Submit yourself therefore to God. Resist the devil and he will flee from you.

   Yield and submit yourself to God. Confess any known sin in your life and ask His cleansing in the Blood of the Lord Jesus Christ.

   Take the authority in the name of Jesus Christ over the devil and his forces, resisting them and commanding them to go. Take the same authority over every contrary spirit, every rebellious nature, every aggressive thought and vain imagination that would exalt itself against God and His Word.

   In prayer, tear down the strongholds that the devil has built up by way of prejudices and barriers in people's minds. The Holy Spirit does this as you pray.

2. **1 Peter 5:6** 'Humble yourself under the mighty hand of God …

   Tell God that you are *humbling* yourself under His mighty hand and that it is not your will but His will that you want to do.

   Tell God that you are *decreasing in order that Jesus may increase* through your life, your witness and your counselling. In doing this you are coming under His line of authority so that His power and authority can run through you to master the situation you are handling.

3. **Ask for the Holy Spirit to anoint you** to uplift the Lord Jesus Christ. Ask Him to drench you in His presence so that you may speak with power and conviction.

4. **Yield to the control of the Holy Spirit.** Tell Him you are giving Him your body, mind, faculties, thought patterns and will, so that He might use you as *His obedient channel*. This means you still make the decisions but you are guided and influenced as to what to do and say. This is the essence of the Spirit-filled life.

5. **Ask the Holy Spirit to release His presence through you** and to minister through you to the people. John 7:37–39.

6. **Ask Him to put His words in your heart, mind and mouth** i.e. to bring to remembrance that which you have read and memorised at the time you are needed to counsel effectively. Ask Him to anoint your lips to speak the way He desires, in words of power, authority, challenge, conviction, life, liberty, love and compassion.

7. **Then thank the Lord for the fact that He has heard and answered your prayers.** Thank Him in terms of the following verses:
   (a) **John 15:16** 'You did not choose Me, but I chose you and appointed you that you should go and bear fruit and that your fruit should remain …'
   (b) **Isaiah 55:11** 'My Word shall not return to me void, but shall accomplish that which I please and prosper in the thing whereto I sent it.'
   (c) **James 4:7** 'Submit yourselves therefore to God, resist the devil and he will flee from you.'

(d) Philippians 2:10–11 'At the name of Jesus every knee should bow and every tongue confess that Jesus is Lord ...' Thank Him that you are submitted to the character and authority of Jesus' name therefore the forces of evil must bow the knee to the authority of Jesus through you as you minister.

(e) Acts 1:8 'And ye shall receive power when the Holy Spirit comes upon you and you shall be My witnesses.'

Thank God that you have the power of the Holy Spirit and the release of His presence through you, therefore you have boldness and power to minister effectively.

(f) John 7:37–39 'If any man is thirsty, let him come to Me and drink ... From his innermost being shall flow rivers of living water ... thus spoke He of the Holy Spirit ...'

Thank God that you have those rivers of living water of the Holy Spirit flowing through you to refresh those to whom you minister.

(g) Acts 4:29–30 'Grant that Thy bondservants may speak Thy Word with all confidence and boldness while Thou dost extend Thy hand to heal and signs and wonders take place through the name of Thy Holy Son Jesus.'

Thank God that because you have asked Him, you are going to speak His Word with confidence and boldness, and He will minister healing and blessings through you in the name of Jesus.

(h) Acts 10:38 'God anointed Jesus with the Holy Spirit and power and He went about doing good and healing all who were oppressed by the devil for God was with Him.'

Thank God that you are anointed by and have the power of the same Holy Spirit that Jesus had, and as a result you are going to do good and heal those who are oppressed by the devil for God is with you too.

(i) John 14:12 'He who believes in Me, the works that I do, shall he do also, and greater works than these shall he do, because I go to the Father.'

Thank God that because Jesus went back to heaven He sent the Holy Spirit to endue you with power to do the works and even greater works than Jesus did, in His name.

(j) Isaiah 50:4 This is a prayer you can pray directly from the Scriptures:

'The Lord God has given me the tongue of the wise and learned so that I should know how to speak a word in season to him that is weary.' (He wakeneth me morning by morning. He wakeneth my ear to hear as the learned. The Lord opened my ear and I was not rebellious neither turned away back.)

It is our responsibility to listen to Him daily from His Word to gain those words of the wise and learned.

Go forth under the authority of the name of Jesus and the power of the Holy Spirit to be His Ambassador in any situation in life.

COUNSELLOR'S INSTRUCTIONS

When counselling an enquirer after an altar call at a mission or crusade, these guidelines can be used when counselling someone personally, and conducting a follow up programme.

SPEND AN UNHURRIED TIME (AT LEAST 10 MINUTES) PRAYING BEFORE YOU COME TO THE MEETING TO BE ABLE TO COUNSEL EFFECTIVELY. ASK GOD TO GIVE YOU HIS WISDOM AS YOU COUNSEL AND RELEASE HIS LOVE THROUGH YOU TO WELCOME THEM INTO THE KINGDOM OF GOD.

1.   You will either lead the person through to the counselling room from the altar call or meet them in the counselling room as you are assigned to them. Smile very warmly as you greet them. Make them feel that you are privileged to know them. Congratulate them very sincerely on their decision to commit their lives to Jesus Christ.

2.   Ascertain the nature of their decision as to whether they are making this decision for the very first time, receiving Christ into their lives, or is it a re-dedication of their lives to Christ. Emphasise to them that both are equally important.

3.   Impress upon them the importance of the decision they have made. If they are receiving Christ, tell them that it has placed them in God's hands and He has:

(a) begun to change their lives here on this earth. (2 Corinthians 5:17)

(b) changed their eternal destination from Hell to Heaven. (John 5:24)

(c) made them someone very special in Christ. (Ephesians 1:6)

(d) made all His blessings and resources available to them as an heir of God. (Romans 8:17)

If they are re-dedicating their lives to Christ, simply re-affirm these things to them. The person has obviously been discouraged, felt rejected and needs to be reassured from God's Word that the Lord has never left them.

4.   Give them the assurance of their position in Christ (point 8 on the instruction sheet, 'How to Lead a Soul to Jesus Christ') i.e. that they are a child of God, have been forgiven and cleansed by the blood of Christ, etc.

5.   Listen to their problems. They may have a very great need. Be patient and a good listener. If they are hypochondriacs and have come only to solicit sympathy, be firm with them and challenge them to make an effort to help themselves by heeding the advice you give them.

6.   Answer their questions as best you can. Don't be side-tracked by irrelevant issues and questions such as creation, the flood, etc. Bring them back to the point

---

of their need, i.e. their commitment to Christ, receiving His salvation, serving Him etc. If you are stumped by a question, call an adviser or leader to help you. Don't be ashamed to tell the person you don't know the answer, but will find out and telephone them or come and see them about it.

7. Challenge them to follow Christ now that they have received Him into their lives. The decision is very important, but it is only the beginning. They must make the effort to follow on with Christ.

8. Give them the Counselling pack or follow-up literature (Gospel of John, Four Spiritual Laws and anything else you may want to include to help them). Get them to fill in a decision card right on the spot to record their decision, for their own benefit.

9. Ask them if they have at least a New Testament. If not, urge them to get one as soon as possible. If they can't afford one, consult your adviser or leader of the mission. It is advisable to have a supply of New Testaments to give to enquirers.

10. Ask them what church they attend. If they are unchurched, recommend a good church in their area. If you don't know one, tell them you will contact them and let them know. Tell them that you will also notify the minister in the area to call upon them.

11. Fill in the COUNSELLING CARD neatly, in every detail. This is for the follow-up programme.

12. Tell them that you are coming to see them and will telephone them to arrange a visit. This is important for they will need reassurance to overcome the doubts that arise.

13. Pray for them that God will bless and help them to follow the Lord Jesus Christ. Pray for any specific needs which they have mentioned that God would meet and supply them in Jesus' name.

14. Take them to a leader or adviser and ask them to share the nature of their decision. When they leave your company, ask them to go to a friend with whom they have come to the service and share the decision with them as well. If they came alone, ask them to call a friend and share it with them as soon as possible.

FOLLOW UP
OF A NEW CHRISTIAN

1.   The very next day ring and make an appointment to come and see them. Be cheerful over the telephone and encourage them briefly to continue with Christ. Tell them you are praying for them.

2.   When visiting them, ask them how they are going on with Christ. Are they having a daily quiet time, i.e. talking to the Lord in prayer and reading His Word? Are they getting anything out of the Scriptures? Do they have any questions about verses of Scripture that might puzzle them? Have they received any answers to prayer as yet? Have they started attending church or at least made enquiries at their local church?

3.   Answer any questions they may have as clearly as possible. Listen to their problems and advise them as best you can, always using the Word of God as your authority. Remember if you don't know the answers, don't stumble around. Tell them so and say that you will find the answer and come back to them.

4.   Pray with them regarding their problems and about going on with Christ.

5.   Start them on a beginners Bible Study course and help them with it, if necessary.

6.   Have a lovely time of fellowship with them. Share your testimony and personal experiences in order to encourage them to continue in their Christian life.

7.   Encourage them again as to whom they are in Christ. (See the next section) Let them know that God is keeping them by His power, and will never fail them.

8.   Make an appointment on the spot to come and see them again in a few days or the following week.

9.   If they are going to attend the same church as you, offer to call for them and take them to church, or at least meet them at the church door to accompany them into the service so they will not feel alone.

10. Be a friend to them in Christ.

WHO YOU ARE IN CHRIST

The Word of God says you are:

1. A child of God (John 1:12).

2. Born again of the Word of God (1 Peter 1:23).

3. Forgiven and washed in the blood of Jesus (Ephesians 1:7; Colossians 1:14; Hebrews 9:14; 1 John 1:9).

4. Saved: from sin and its consequences (Romans 10:13; Ephesians 2:8–9).

5. A new creation in Christ (2 Corinthians 5:17).

6. Delivered from satan's kingdom into God's kingdom (Colossians 1:13).

7. Redeemed from the curse of the Law (Galatians 3:13; 1 Peter 1:18).

8. More than a conqueror through Jesus (Romans 8:37).

9. A joint heir through Jesus Christ (Romans 8:17).

10. Accepted in the Beloved (Ephesians 1:6).

11. Complete in Christ (Colossians 2:10).

12. Alive with Christ (Ephesians 2:5).

13. Free from condemnation (Romans 8:1).

14. A partaker of God's divine nature (2 Peter 1:4).

15. Able to do all things in Christ Jesus (Philippians 4:13).

16. Set free from all bondage (John 8:31, 32 & 36).

17. Crucified with Christ (dead to sin and alive to Him) (Galatians 2:20).

18. An ambassador of Christ (2 Corinthians 5:20).

19. Being changed more and more into His image (2 Corinthians 3:18; Philippians 1:6).

20. Raised up with Christ and seated in heavenly places of blessing (Ephesians 2:6).

21. A temple of the Holy Spirit (1 Corinthians 6:19–20).

22. A fellow citizen with the Saints and of the household of God (Ephesians 2:19).

23. Qualified to share in His inheritance (Colossians 1:12).

24. Christ's possession (1 Corinthians 3:23).

SHARING A TESTIMONY CORRECTLY

There are 3 main elements in a testimony
Share them concisely without waffling:

1. Events leading to commitment to Jesus
2. How you made the commitment – in detail
3. Share one or two up-to-date blessings to show Jesus is still relevant today

Spend more time on 2 and 3, than on part 1.

Giving a testimony can be:
• Sowing seeds • Watering • Reaping

To Whom:
• Christians and the Unsaved

To Produce:
• Salvation • Healing • Deliverance • Baptism in the Holy Spirit etc.

Mark Chapter 4
The Parable of the sower and the seed
We must sow the *Word of God* with our testimony – Hebrews 4:12. God's Word is 'alive and powerful'.

Our testimony does not 'quicken' – it warms or inspires. But the Word of God 'quickens' and draws people to Jesus.

Quote the Word of God – i.e. John 3:16, John 1:12, 2 Corinthians 5:17, John 6:47.

What you Sow is what you Reap
To get people saved – testimony on Salvation
To get people healed – testimony on Healing
To get people baptised in the Holy Spirit – testimony on Baptism in the Holy Spirit
To get people delivered – testimony on Deliverance
Your testimony encourages people to trust God.

Next to God's Word nothing carries more weight than your personal testimony.

POINTS FOR PUBLIC SPEAKING

Preach to Get Results

1. **What is your motive when you preach or share?**

   (a) To increase your popularity?

   (b) To bring people to Christ?

2. **Preach what God gives you.**

   (a) Don't worry about offending the carnal mind.

   (b) Don't be concerned about what your hearers will say – as they said to Jesus 'This is a hard saying who can hear it?'

3. **Make clear distinct points.**
   Don't fear for the Word to disturb their consciences they need to be alarmed about their souls.

4. **Teaching Techniques.**

   (a) Use good illustrations.

   (b) Use interesting ways to repeat important statements.

   (c) Emphasise main points by good choice of words and varying tone of your voice. These will help hearers to remember your message.

5. **Don't appeal mainly to their emotions.**
   Challenge their consciences with the Word (2 Timothy 4:1–4).

6. **Testify from your own personal experiences** (1 Corinthians 2:1–5) of the power of the Gospel/Word, this will bring conviction that you have something they need.

7. **Don't worry about awakening in the hearers uncomfortable memories by reminding them of unrepented sins.**

   (a) The devil doesn't mind if we denounce sin in general.

   (b) Challenge specific sin (that could be prevalent in the crowd).

8. **Challenge them to obey the Truth at once.**

   (a) Delayed obedience is disobedience.

   (b) Be strong enough to present God's command and press gently for immediate response.

   (c) Expect them to commit themselves on the spot.

9.   Don't leave them with the impression they are expected to go away in their sins and consider the matter at leisure – D.L. Moody, 8 October 1871. Moody did not give altar calls and many left that Sunday night only to perish in the Great Fire of Chicago. Moody regretted letting them out of his presence without calling them to a commitment to Christ. This changed his life and ministry after which he always urged people to a commitment.

10.   Don't let them think they are unable to obey or that they must wait for God to move them or change them.

    (a)   Change will come when they commit their lives to Jesus.

    (b)   Lead them to Him now.

11.   Let them know that Salvation is a Gift from God!

    (a)   Point out that they are unsaved and condemned unless they repent (John 3:36).

    (b)   They are lost and in terrible danger.

    (c)   They will then understand how much they need Salvation.

12.   Preach the Gospel as a remedy.

    (a)   But don't conceal the disease.

    (b)   It is fatal! The result is eternal death in hell!

OPEN AIR MINISTRY

Deuteronomy 31:12 – God's Plan for Evangelism

Assemble the people, the *men*, *women*, and *children* and the *alien* who is in your town, in order that they may *hear* and *learn* and *fear the Lord* your God and be *careful to observe* all the words of this law.

Open Air Ministry

– people seeing the church (local) in action – (they SEE the church in their city).
– Sharing faith in Christ in a DYNAMIC, PRACTICAL, ATTRACTIVE, VISUAL WAY.

Use Visual Aids:

EZEKIEL – shaved off half his beard/made models in streets of Babylon – communicated God's message through visual aids, street-drama etc. (1440 pagan temples – One man with God's message).

HABAKKUK – used a sketch board (clay tablets). God says 'write my message clearly.'

JESUS – Every 9 times preached – 7 outdoors using visual aids from every day life!

Five senses to take in information every day:
3% through smell, 3% through taste, 6% through feeling, 13% through ears, and 75% through eyes.
If stand in pulpit and preach – aiming at 13% of receptivity,
but if preach and use visual aids – aiming at 88% of receptivity.

USE VISUAL AIDS – Arouse People's God-Given Curiosity!

Tips for Open Air Ministry

1. **Prayer**, intercession and worship – privately beforehand
2. **Aim** – uplift Jesus, explain Gospel, bring people to Christ
(NOT a worship service.)
3. **Strategic place** – where people are/gather
    – movie crowds
    – bus stops
    – shopping area
    • Scripture billboards – advertise
    • Regular times – each Saturday morning.
4. **PA System?** NO – unless very big crowd or very noisy area
Danger – people stand afar off – need to draw them close!
5. **Music** – instruments (guitars, etc.)
Joyful outreach songs – keep eyes open when singing – eye contact with people

6. **Song items** – good, sharp, outreach items
7. **Street theatre**
    – clown skits, one-man plays
    – short, to the point Gospel plays
    – pointing to Jesus!
    – puppets, ventriloquist dolls, etc
    – sketch board art messages (one man can do this)
8. **Testimonies** – short, clear, filled with Scripture – salvation (healing, deliverance – 'bell' to draw people)
    (a) life before conversion
    (b) how made commitment
    (c) difference Jesus has made (Paul – Acts 26 to Agrippa)
9. **Short message**
    – filled with Word (re salvation)
    – to hold attention
    – sow seeds as hearer is walking from points A–B in front of the presentation
10. **Co-ordinate programme**
    – not disjointed
    – planned, know what you're going to do next
11. **Counsellors in crowd** (looking anonymous)
    – Stand with curious people
    – ask 'What do you think?' 'Where do you fit in?'
    – Good tracts and literature to give
    – Be bold – nothing to lose
    – Get particulars for visitation
12. **Appeal**
    – give altar call
    – ask to pray in crowd with you
    – amazing willingness after prayer
    – ask for show of hands (counsellors link up with them)
    – ask to step forward and take stand for Christ
13. **Break** – Half an hour for counselling (or one hour)
    – START AGAIN TO FRESH CROWD!

Can Have:

– Children's programme
– parents will come out to see as well
– Take whole *church service* outdoors – people will gravitate out of curiosity
Luke 14:23 – 'Go into highways and byways ...'

OPEN AIR WORK = WITNESS – CONTACT – SOUL-WINNING – BRINGING FOLK INTO LOCAL CHURCH

WINNING YOUR FAMILY

Ephesians 5:18 says, 'Be filled with the Spirit.' How can people tell you are filled with the Holy Spirit? There are many theological answers one could give, but the most practical demonstration is when you're under pressure. Picture an unmarked tube. How do you know what's in it? By squeezing it of course! When you squeeze it the contents are forced out. When you're squeezed by pressure what comes out – impatience, tension, stress, frustration, unpleasantness? But if the graciousness and sweetness of God's spirit flows out, that's what you are filled with. You see, being filled with God's Spirit also means staying filled with Him and living under His influence and control. The place where you experience the most pressure is in your home. Your life, filled with the Holy Spirit, is the most powerful means of witnessing in your home.

Ephesians 5:21 to 6:4 – gives guidelines for husbands, wives and children to be the most effective witnesses in their home.

Husbands

Love your wife and be prepared to die to preserve and secure her. Just as Christ loved the church – that much! Do you want your wife to submit to you as head of the home? Then love her that way and give her the security she needs and God expects. If you don't, don't expect her to submit. If Christ did not love the church, would you submit to Him as your Lord? Husband, you are the head of your home, not as a dictator or tyrant, but as a loving shepherd, providing for your wife and children in every possible way – spiritually, mentally, psychologically and socially and guarding them by your Godly example.

If your wife and children are not saved *don't nag or pressurise them*, show them by a strong and loving example what Christ has done for you. Pray for them and gently encourage them. Remember how long it took for you to come to the Lord.

Don't cut your wife off because she's not a Christian, she's still your wife and lover. *See her as a potential Christian* and tactfully share your friendship with Jesus with her.

Don't provoke your children to anger by being pushy. You still have to discipline them. While they are living under your roof, they must still obey the rules of the home. Setting standards and providing guidelines for them will show them your love.

Wives

Wife submit to your husband as you do to the Lord, even if your husband is unsaved, he is still the head of your home in God's eyes. The moment you look down on him because he's not saved, you bring disorder into your home and frustrate God's purposes. Instead *exalt your husband to the headship* of the home and encourage him regarding decisions, guidance and provision (even though you may be the one making the decisions, tactfully suggest them to him and let him think they came from him).

Don't nag him to become a Christian. Don't leave tracts under his pillow etc. 1 Peter 3:1–4 shows how you may *win your husband by the inner beauty of Christ* in your life, your loving example and your respect for your husband – and all this without a word of nagging or pressure. Nothing drives a man away like a wife nagging him to become a Christian. He'll see his need of Christ by your beautiful relationship with Jesus.

Remember you are still his wife and lover – be that to him, don't cut him off as a second grade human being. He's not, he's the man you pledged to love and cherish. When you release him to his place as head of the home and be his wife, you'll find that God will reach into his heart and convince him of his need of Christ far more effectively than your words can. Of course, take the opportunities you get, especially when he asks, to lovingly share what Jesus is doing for you. Don't degrade or belittle him as you do this, but gently urge him to receive Jesus as you did.

Teenagers and children

Ephesians 6:1–3 says, 'Children obey your parents ... honour your father and mother ... that it may go well with you and that you may enjoy long life ...'.

Honouring your father and mother even though they may not seem honourable to you and obeying them is the most powerful witness of Christ you can ever show. Let them see that Christ has made you a better, more obedient son or daughter. Do things immediately when you are told or asked to, even look for things that need attending to, before you're asked. That may surprise or shock them, but it will certainly speak deeply to their hearts. With the help of Christ, maintain that witness and let them see your relationship with Jesus is a lasting one.

Stay in submission to your parents, obey them when they set rules and regulations for you (even if you think they're unfair). If they're unreasonable, talk with them lovingly about it but don't argue bitterly, that will put up barriers between you and drive them away from receiving Christ. Far better to submit to them and win them to Christ, than win the argument and drive them away.

Use your opportunities very tactfully and gently to *talk to them about Christ*. Don't talk down to them or belittle them even though you may know more about Christ than they do. The quickest way to win your folks is to respect them for the knowledge they have and encourage them to open their lives to Christ. They may even ask you about it all. Take it easy and don't pressurise them, they're not where you are yet. When they do receive Christ, encourage them to grow in Him, but don't push, be patient. God has been very patient with you too.

In all three categories, *pray earnestly* for the unsaved members of your home, and love them into a relationship with Jesus.

To make this sort of difference in your home, you need to be the person, with Christ's help, to *break down walls and barriers* and be the first to reach out to others in your home.

Practical Steps to Break Down Barriers and Heal Relationships
Six little sentences to have operative in your life:

1.   'I love you'
Easy to say, but another thing to make sure the other person feels loved by you. *You* show the love, even though *they're* not showing it. The most practical way to show your love is by *staying home* – being there to let them feel your love instead of being out all the time. Our love for our family is spelt T.I.M.E. – *time spent with them*. Take time to get to know them – their likes, dislikes, fears and needs. You might find a very lonely, needy person there that you never knew before.

Treat your family with respect in front of other people, husbands honour your wives in public, don't belittle or ignore them, and wives, vice versa. Teenagers and children, honour your parents before others and don't reject them. Parents don't embarrass your children, or expect too much of them. Take an interest in what they're doing, or what interests them.

YOUR LOVE FOR YOUR FAMILY
1 Corinthians 13:4–7 (paraphrase)

> 'My love for my family is very patient and kind. Never jealous or envious. It is never boastful or proud. It is never haughty, or selfish, or rude.
> My love for my family does not demand its own way, it is not irritable, or touchy.
> My love for my family does not hold grudges and will hardly even notice when other family members do it wrong. It is never glad about injustice, but rejoices whenever truth wins out.
> If I love my family I will be loyal to them no matter what the cost. I will always believe in them, always expect the best of them and always stand my ground in defending them.'

Your family members will respond to you and to the Lord according to how you treat them.

2.   'Thank you'
Look for the things your family members are doing right and acknowledge them, especially the things they do for you. Overlook or gently correct the things that

are wrong without criticising or harping on them. Focus on the things you can be grateful for and not on the things you despise.

Saying 'thank you' to your family members is like giving the best form of reward you can. They'll respond to you positively again and again. Ephesians 4:29 'Do not let any unwholesome talk come out of your mouth, but only that which is useful for building others up.' Don't wait for your family to thank you first. You take the initiative and build them up through your gratitude and appreciation. Don't wait till their funeral to say edifying and beautiful things about them. Let them know now – they'll appreciate it far more.

3. 'How Do You Feel?'
James 1:19 'Be quick to listen, slow to speak and slow to anger.' Obey this verse in your home, listen to them. Try to feel what they're feeling. 'Walk a mile in their shoes' and try to experience what they're going through. Be a good listener in your home and you'll find out many things about your family that will give you a point of contact to win them.

Teenagers – Realise that your parents aren't perfect. They learnt from imperfect parents and one day you'll be an imperfect parent. Without Christ's help you'll never manage. You need to love them to Christ by being understanding and compassionate.

Remember too that *your parents are trying to protect you* from situations they think are going to hurt or destroy you. Perhaps circumstances have changed since they were young, but the principles of danger are the same. They probably have a little more foresight than you do. Listen to them before you respond in anger at what you think is over-protection. Try to understand where they're coming from. You may learn some wonderful things as a result.

When you think your *parents are being critical* of your seeming failures, instead of complimenting you for your successes, realise that they *want you to improve*. They want you to be better and more successful than they were. See this as love and concern on their part.

Include them as much as possible in your life and activities. They've invested so much in you. They may be a little pushy, but understand where they're coming from. They love you and want to be part of your life, let them in, don't be ashamed of them. Offer to include them occasionally in your activities and plans. Share with them what your plans are, let them know how your day has gone, enquire how they have fared. *Ask their opinion* whether you need it or not, just as a bridge of communication. It will show them you have confidence in their experience.

4. 'I Forgive you'
Ephesians 4:32 'Be kind and compassionate to one another, forgiving each other, just as, in Christ, God forgave you.' Maybe you've been hurt, abandoned,

disappointed, let down or abused. You need to forgive; you can't do this on your own you need to come to the cross and acknowledge 'Jesus you forgave those who hurt me through your death and shed blood. You live in me, therefore, please give me the grace to forgive those who've hurt me.' Then by an act of your will, say to God, 'I forgive them' (mention their names). Then ask God to forgive you for your bitterness, and heal your attitude. If you don't you'll carry that bitterness as poison in you for the rest of your life, that will contaminate and destroy your life, your marriage, your children, your relationships and everything you're involved in.

Realise you've probably hurt those who have hurt you and they need to forgive you too, but you take the initiative and forgive first. *Unforgiveness towards anyone is the greatest single barrier that hinders your fellowship with God*. That's the worst thing that could happen to you. Do you see how unforgiveness and bitterness hurts you more than anyone else? It's not worth it. Ephesians 4:26 says, 'Do not let the sun go down on your anger.' Don't let your bitterness carry over into another day, make it right now.

5. 'I was wrong'

James 5:16 'Confess your faults one to another and pray for one another that you may be healed.' 'I was wrong' are the three most healing words in the human language. *If you're wrong – admit it*; don't be the person who believes they're always right. That person is so frustrating to be with, especially when you know they're wrong. It doesn't matter who is right, but what is right. If you're wrong, admit that the other person is right. Heal the relationship and make it right, even if you're only 10% wrong in the situation, admit it and build the bridge to heal the relationship. Jesus would do this if He were in the situation, and He is there in you.

6. 'I need help'

Ephesians 5:21 'Submit to one another out of reverence for Christ' (referring to family relationships). Be willing to learn, go to your family and explain that there are attitudes and habits you have that you really want to change and ask them to help you. You know that God put your family together for the purpose of loving and helping each other. Watch the walls melt as you do this. Above all this, know that you need God's help. Always keep open to Him and sensitive to His correction and guidance.

Your family relationship is the most precious of all human relationships. If you'll let Jesus touch and heal you in this area, *He'll heal you of the 'cancer' of selfishness* that is destroying families everywhere. This 'cancer' demands 'me first, my way, my needs and blow anyone else'. The only way to deal with this 'cancer' is to come to the Lord and admit that you're plagued with this affliction. Acknowledge that He died and paid the price for it and call on Him to heal and set you free from the 'cancer' of selfishness. Even if you're the only one in your family who's able to say, 'Lord, I'm available to be the unselfish person in my

---

home. I'll consider others first and put myself last. Start the healing process in my home through me.'

If your family members have moved to other locations write them a letter as a bridge of communication, using these six sentences as a skeleton outline.

Can you imagine the changes God will effect in your home through you? You may not see results immediately, but they will materialise and you'll have the most fantastic opportunity of all to share Christ with them. They'll be seeing Him in operation through you like no other way possible. He'll make such an impact on them through you and you'll see everlasting results. Your family needs Jesus living in your home and the only way he's going to do it is through you. As well as this, you will have perfected, as much as possible, through practice the ideal way of conducting yourself in a family.

HOW TO WIN YOUR FRIENDS TO CHRIST

Proverbs 18:24 'A man that hath friends must show himself friendly: and there is a friend that sticketh closer than a brother.'

If you are a true friend and are genuinely concerned for your friends you'll want them to go to heaven too. YOUR LIFE IS YOUR MOST POWERFUL WEAPON in influencing friends to Christ. It speaks far more loudly than words from your mouth, in fact, it backs up your words very powerfully.

Here are three factors to help you to reach your friends in a positive way:

1. The Freshness Factor
Remember you are sharing your relationship with Jesus, therefore keep it fresh and natural.

Don't talk about your beliefs about Christ or Christianity, but share how the relationship you have with Him has changed your life.

When witnessing talk about the difference your 'Friend' makes in your life, i.e. when you're lonely, depressed, frustrated, or hurt. You have a friend who makes the difference.

Make sure your relationship with Jesus is fresh and vital. If it's stale then there's something wrong. Some barrier you need to remove is hindering your friendship.

Our message should be, 'I have a friend who's changing me and carrying me through the down times. He's a friend who's helping me make my decisions. I have a fresh, exciting relationship with Him'.

They don't need your beliefs, they need your friend.

2. The Focus Factor
Focus in on one friend at a time; that's the way to begin winning the world to Christ.

There is *some person* without Christ who you're closer to than any other Christian is. You may be the only one whom God is counting on to reach that friend. Write their name on a card and stick it into your Bible. Each day bring them to the Lord in prayer.

Focus your prayers and energies on bringing that person to Christ. You have a mission, a full time ministry to reach that person.

Stay in shape spiritually. Keep your life yielded to Christ so that your friend can see and experience Him through you.

3. The Friendship Factor

Your friend ought be getting a better friend in you, because of your relationship with Jesus.

Do they see in you the most loyal, caring, listening, sensitive, helpful friend they've ever had?

The bridge between them and Jesus is the kind of friend you are thus you will win the right to speak to them about Christ.

Remember the special days in your friend's life, i.e. birthday – send them a card/put a birthday poster in their office, or a flower on their desk/take or send some flowers to them.

Let them know they're special to you and they'll realise they're special to Jesus.

Be there when they're down or experiencing a crisis. Be available and caring when they're experiencing financial, family or relationship troubles. Look for ways to show you care.

1 Peter 3:15 – 'Be always ready to give a reason for the hope that is in you, with *gentleness and respect*.'

When you share Christ with a friend, they should feel bigger, not smaller; respected not belittled.

Are you prepared to be the best friend your friend has ever had so that they can be your friend forever in heaven?

Tips for talking to your friends about Christ:

Go ask their opinion about something e.g. a Christian record, or an article that presents Christ. Lend it to them, asking them to bring it back with their opinion. When they've told you their opinion, don't belittle them, but tell them yours about the 'Friend' who's made the difference in your life.

Invite them to a meeting, if they don't make a decision, use the message as a talking point. You've been given a wonderful opportunity.

Pray about talking to your friend

1.　Lord give me a *natural opportunity* to start talking about Jesus to my friend (name your friend to God).

2.　Lord, when you do, help me to *recognise the opportunity*. Lord, I'm expecting you to do it.

3. When I recognise it, give me the *courage to use the opportunity*.

When you next see your friend, be on the lookout for the open door which you know God is going to give you. Don't be frightened, God will have been preparing their hearts as a result of your prayers.

What to say to your friend

2 Corinthians 5: 14–21 gives us the message of reconciliation to share:

1. There is a relationship you were meant to have. You can't be happy and have peace without it.

2. That relationship with God was ruined. We ruined it because we left Him and did our own thing (we rebelled and sinned). Sin separates us from God that's why our lives are full of gaps. Those gaps are there because the things God wants to put there, are not there yet.

3. That relationship has the potential to be restored because Jesus paid the price for all the laws we broke. His blood satisfied God's righteous judgement on sin. He paid in full the account we had with God, which we were unable to pay.

4. Like any relationship, you've got to respond to it. You can't have a one way love relationship. Jesus is reaching out saying 'I paid the price for you, I love you.' You've got to reach out to Him in return.

That's what winning a friend to Christ is. It's all about a relationship – not about a belief or religion – a relationship/friendship day by day with Jesus.

YOUR FRIEND DOESN'T HAVE TO PERISH BECAUSE SOMEONE IS CLOSE ENOUGH TO RESCUE THEM – YOU!

WINNING JEWISH PEOPLE TO THE MESSIAH

In His earthly life, the Lord Jesus Christ was Jewish. 'But when the fulness of the time had come, God sent forth His Son, born of a woman, born under the Law ... (Galatians 4:4). God has such a beautiful plan for the nation of Israel and desires with all His heart that they should come to the Messiah, Jesus. Paul in Romans 10:1 expressed the desire of Father's heart when he said, 'Brethren, my heart's desire and prayer for Israel is that they might be saved.' While God has prophetic plans for Israel as a nation, it is still His desire for Jewish men, women and children to receive the Messiah Jesus. He wants to use us to fulfil this plan.

However, with Jewish folk, the direct, confrontational approach does not usually work. We need to win their confidence and friendship, and let them see the characteristics of the Messiah in us. Jesus was never pushy with the needy Jewish folk around Him. He was gentle and kind, and met them at their point of need. We have to be the same if we are to win them to the Messiah.

You see that, although Jesus was a Jew, He was a gentleman. Usually Jews snubbed the Samaritans who lived in Palestine; however, Jesus spoke and ministered to a sinful woman at the well of Sychar in Samaria. He was courteous and kind as He offered her Living Water. Although He was Jewish, she acknowledged Him as a gentleman, for she addressed Him as 'Sir'. In John 4:11, when Jesus revealed her sinful past, she realised that this Jewish Gentleman was also a prophet. By the time Jesus revealed that He was the Messiah in verse 26, she was ready, not only to acknowledge Him thus, but also to declare that fact to the whole town. As a result they came to the Messiah as well.

As always, our lives are our greatest weapon in witnessing. The Holy Spirit in us desires to make us more like Jesus. Galatians 5:22, 23 tells us about 'the fruit of the Spirit = love, joy, peace, patience, kindness, goodness, faithfulness, gentleness and self-control.' These are the characteristics of the Messiah that the Holy Spirit desires to produce in our lives. According to Psalm 34:8, others are invited to 'taste and see that the Lord is good.' One of the finest ways to draw anyone into a relationship with Jesus is to let them enjoy the fruit of the Spirit that we bear. When people, especially Jewish people, see these characteristics of Messiah in our lives they will know that He is alive and real.

The starting point in getting close to Jewish people is to *become a friend. When they are in need*, let them know that you are praying for them and really seeking God for solutions on their behalf. When they have family problems, or their children are ill, you will find that they will come to you and ask for prayer. A marvellous point of contact is to *remember their feasts, fasts and celebrations*. Buy them an appropriate card, a gift. Even offer to go to synagogue occasionally with them on a Friday evening. They may even invite you to their children's bar mitzvahs or bat mitzvahs when they come of age at thirteen. If you can help it, don't ever refuse those invitations. They are honouring you very highly by sharing these holy family occasions with you. You and the Messiah in you have really started to 'get into their hearts'.

EQUIPPED TO GO!

Here are some wonderful tips to love your Jewish friends to the Messiah and win you opportunities to speak of Him. Remember the letters of the word PROMISES. They will help you in this delightful task.

P – Pray for God to work in their hearts by His Holy Spirit. Pray that He will convict them of their need of the Messiah and they will desire what they see of Him in you.

R – Refrain from doing and saying things that will drive them away. For instance, do not imitate Jewish accents. Do not crack Jewish jokes; they have had enough sarcastic criticism. Do not drop names of notable Jewish people you know; this does not impress them. Do not use the word 'Jew'; it is used too derogatorily, rather say 'Jewish people'. Avoid arguments about details of Christian doctrine, such as the Trinity and the Virgin Birth. Rather let them recognize who the Messiah is and what He has done in you.

O – Old Testament is the area of Scripture they understand. Write down a few Old Testament verses for them pertaining to the Messiah, such as Isaiah 53:1–6, Isaiah 7:14 and 9:6, Zechariah 9:9. Then, as you win their confidence, get them to read, if they will, the Gospel of John, informing them that John was Jewish. He was not anti-Semitic at all. Many astute Orthodox Jewish people will ask how, if Jesus is our Messiah and the whole Old Testament is about Him, how come His name is never mentioned in it even once. You can answer them very gently and lovingly by informing them that it is, approximately one hundred times from Genesis to Habakkuk: the name 'Yeshua' (Jesus).

Wherever the Old Testament word SALVATION, especially preceded by the possessive pronoun *My*, *Thy*, or *His* is found, it is the identical word for 'Yeshua', which means 'Jehovah is Salvation'. Do you recall the statements that the angel Gabriel used in Luke 1:31 to Mary, and Matthew 1:21 to Joseph, when he told them that they should call His name 'Jesus for He would save His people from their sins'? Remember that the angel did not speak in English, Latin or Greek, but in Hebrew, and neither Mary nor Joseph failed to grasp the meaning and significance of this Name in relation to the Messiah's character and work of salvation. He came to save the world through His Son. A few magnificent passages that reveal this name are Habakkuk 3:13, Isaiah 12:2 & 3, 62:11.

Do you remember when Simeon in Luke 2:29–30 was holding the baby Jesus in his arms said, 'Lord, now lettest Thy servant depart in peace ... for mine eyes have seen Thy ('Yeshua') salvation'? There was that word again; wherever it was preceded by a possessive pronoun, that refers to Jesus. We cannot get away from it.

M – Messianic prophecies are found right throughout the Old Testament. Use the word, 'Messiah', rather than 'Christ'. It means the same in the Hebrew language. Even though they may not believe the word of God, it is alive and powerful and will work in their hearts, so quote it anyway from passages such as Micah 5:2 regarding his birth, Isaiah 53:5 and 6 regarding His death, Zechariah 13:6 regarding His wounds and Psalm 22 in connection with His suffering. All these passages unmistakably point to the Messiah Jesus.

I – Israel: Christians should have a sympathy for the plight of Israel. This does not mean that we should get involved in political arguments, but we should show a concern for this nation which God loves dearly. They have had a traumatic past, and are very touched when we show them sympathetic concern.

S – Show the love of Jesus. Basically it is not solid doctrine or good sermons that wins people, especially Jewish people, but love. Show this love by inviting them to meals, such as church dinners, rather than services that will frighten them. You will be amazed how they will open up when you sit them down and serve them food. A loving witness that fumbles around will win them far more effectively than an eloquent, argumentative witness. It helps to know a few Jewish words to communicate with them, such as:

Shalom – Peace (they value this word dearly)

Mazel Tov – Congratulations

Chaver shelli – My friend

E – Educate yourself on Jewish history and customs. You do not have to know all eighty volumes of the Talmud, but some good literature on Jewish customs, history and ceremonies will find them very impressed at your interest. Why not ask them to explain a few customs which you do not understand? They will be thrilled to do this.

S – Share your own faith in the Messiah. Do not pulverise them with the Gospel by saying 'You need my Christ'. Rather use the gentler approach, 'I believe in **your** Messiah. He has forgiven and saved me.' That is a marvellous witness and will probably provoke them to ask themselves whether they believe in their Messiah.

Do not push or pressurise them into a commitment. They have so many doubts to overcome first and questions to be answered. Continue to be available to them and be a friend. Introduce them to other loving, gentle followers of the Messiah. When they have received Jesus into their lives and yielded to His Lordship, be very careful and gentle with your follow-up methods. They may still be very suspicious and apprehensive about committing themselves to a Christian community, mainly out of fear of their Jewish family and friends. Personal visits are the ideal start where you can encourage them personally. Then involve them in fun activities with other Christians, such as church picnics, sporting activities, concerts, or Christian business functions. Lead them gently, step by step into a home fellowship group and then into the fuller life of the local church. Your patience will be well rewarded because when a Jewish person comes to Christ, they learn to count the cost (and it is a great cost); they will stand as firm as a rock.

EVERYDAY OPPORTUNITIES TO SHARE CHRIST

Remember God uses ordinary people – He works through you and me. Don't say 'I'm too timid', you know Jesus personally as your Lord and Saviour; you have His Holy Spirit living in you to fill and endue you with power; you *can* witness anywhere.

If You're Timid

– Wear a badge – 'Jesus loves you' or a lapel emblem – a cross or a fish or a '?'. These attract attention and give you an opportunity to speak.
– Keep a Bible on your desk at work.
– Tract distribution – use a good tract on the street or bus, train, aeroplane, etc.

Use Opportunities Well

Use natural opportunities as spiritual points of contact:
– On a bus or aeroplane when asked, 'What's your final destination?' – the answer 'Heaven'. It will open the conversation.
– In a news agency – put a tract in a magazine.
– Through the mail – advertisements come with prepaid postage envelopes put a tract in the envelope and send it back.
– When paying accounts, put a tract with the payment (not when overdue of course).

Your Home – A Fantastic Place for Evangelism

– A tract rack or table at the door.
– Door to door salesman – let him speak about his product, then you speak about Jesus. Give him a tract and witness.
– Repairmen coming to fix appliances – set out tea and cake and give a tract and witness.
– Cassette tape player breaks down – send to repair shop with Gospel tape in it.

Telephone

Great for witnessing
– When answering the phone, be cheerful, use Gospel phrases.
– Put a cheerful Gospel greeting on your answering machine.
– When leaving a message on somebody else's answering machine, bless them in the name of the Lord, leave a Gospel greeting.
– Use God-glorifying words, i.e. 'God bless you', 'Jesus loves you'.

Use Telephone Directory

– Start at 'A' and call everyone with the message, 'God's burdened me to call you to let you know He loves you. Do you have a need? Can I pray for you? What's your relationship with Jesus?'

– You could start a fellowship from all the people you call and minister to.
– Advertise a mission – divide up the telephone book to people in the congregation, get them to call people, ask if they have needs, lead them to Jesus.

Home Evangelistic Outreach

– Invite folk around to have a meal or tea and watch a Gospel video.
– Your children invite other children or teenagers around, play games, table tennis, show film or video, lead them to Jesus.
– Arrange Bible studies to help them grow.

Be a Blessing
Where Tragedies/Disasters/Deaths/Arrests Take Place
Check newspaper reports that give addresses:
– Write to the bereaved and those in need – be gentle and kind, not judgemental.
– Send a tract with a loving letter, endeavour to lead them to Jesus.
– Ask if you can visit them, let them know you care.

Hitch-Hikers

– Fill your car up with them – of course be led by the Lord as to who you should pick up. In your car you have a right to speak to them.

Collect People for Church

– Elderly people, teenagers from a home. Don't come to church with only one person in the car. Stop at the roadside and pick up people.

Your Neighbourhood

– Invite neighbours to a barbeque – invite a preacher or singer along; sing a few songs, have a short message, lead them to Jesus.

Have an Unsaved/Saved Rally

– Invite a well-known speaker and tell Christians they're not allowed in unless they bring an unsaved person.
– If they can't find someone to bring, let them drive the streets and pick people up.

Other Places to Witness

– **Petrol Station** – give tracts to the attendants; talk to them about Jesus.
– **Restaurants** – leave tracts among the paper serviettes.
– **Public toilets** – leave a tract in a visible place.

– **Laundromat** – people sit around depressed; housewives and screaming children; unhappy teenagers; very lonely people. Put tracts in the romantic magazines, etc.
– **Waiting rooms** – of doctors, dentists, hairdressing salons, etc. Place your used Gospel literature and magazines in those strategic places.
– **Restaurants** – when waiter/waitress hands you the menu, leave a tract with 'Here's a lovely spiritual menu for you'.

Personal Commitment to Witness

We need to make a commitment to witness regularly:

– **EACH DAY** to one new person
– **EACH WEEK** – on a specific night just for outreach – vary the place – hospital, old folks home, on streets, door to door, children's home, etc.

Without a commitment, we never make the effort.

Follow Up

Do as much follow up as possible at the time you lead people to Christ as you may not see them again. Leave adequate literature. Get their name, address and phone number for yourself or someone else to visit them. Have a group of approximately 25 people whom you are visiting and witnessing to strongly; lead them to Jesus; train them to win others. Keep the witnessing cycle going, i.e. reach a man, then his wife, children, friends, etc.

We must constantly reach out, if we don't our outreach or church will stagnate.

Mix with unsaved people regularly to witness, otherwise you'll only meet with your saved friends and have no one to witness to.

Pattern of Witnessing

Look at your life, see if there's a pattern of people being converted. Allow the Lord to use you with this vision, day by day, seeking in any situation you're in; for the passion to bring people to God. Being a soul winner is for all of us – 'Do the work of an evangelist'.

It's more blessed to give than receive; we receive so much – 'freely you have received, freely give'. How about giving out the Good News of Jesus regularly?

The Secret of Your Joy

When you lead people to Jesus, there is 'rejoicing in heaven over one sinner that repents'. The Holy Spirit causes joy in heaven – He is in you and will cause that joy to abound in you as well.

See the Eternal Being There

Our souls live forever, they're eternal. Go for the person's soul to win them to Christ (don't forget to make them a follower of Jesus as well). The only thing we can take to heaven is people, invest yourself, your time, your talents, your resources, your spare money, in bringing people to Jesus and help others to bring people to Jesus as well.

Pray for

'All men everywhere' (1 Timothy 2:4) to be saved, for 'God is not willing that any should perish, but that all should come to repentance.'

And also

'Pray that the Lord of the harvest will thrust forth labourers into the harvest' (Luke 10:2, Matthew 9:38).

'Harvest is plenteous but labourers are few' – that's the problem – people are ready for harvesting, but there are so few labourers. If we just explain things simply to them and ask them to receive Jesus, most would get saved. Don't underestimate God, you're working with the Holy Spirit, just give Him the opportunity to use you.

We Need to Yield to the Lord Now

Ask Him to burden your heart to seek and win the lost:

To baptise you with fire (the Holy Spirit and fire) the fire that purges, unctionises, brings conviction.

To give you His passion for the lost.

A Commitment Brings Liberty and Release

As long as we're just thinking about it, we'll still be uncertain and have no release. We'll be hindered and inhibited. Yield to the Lord to work with Him and fulfil the cause that is the dearest to His heart, seek a new anointing from Him for 'it is the anointing of the Holy Spirit that breaks the yoke.' We need to sell out to Jesus to seek and save the lost.

WRITING YOUR PERSONAL TRACT

When you write your testimony it's like going into the witness stand for Jesus. People don't want just to know about you. They really want to hear about what you know of Jesus. These brief notes may help you put your personal tract together:

1. Pray:

Ask Jesus what He wants you to say and how He wants it said.

2. Choose:

In the space available you're not going to be able to fit it all in. Decide on your aim – to challenge, to encourage, to explain. Then choose one aspect of Jesus' work in your life – conversion, family life, financial provision, freedom from fear, being filled with the Spirit.

3. Talk:

It's good to talk about your testimony to someone who knows you to check what you want to say makes sense. Don't be afraid to ask for help with writing, and do get someone to look it over when you've written it. Can they recognise you in it?

4. Write:

It's important to tell your story in your way, but I've found these things helpful:

Avoid jargon: e.g. 'God has been good to me', not 'The Lord has blessed me'.

Be specific: e.g. 'God healed my asthma', not 'felt the healing touch of God'.

Use short sentences: They keep people's attention.

Keep to the point: Don't wander off into the unimportant.

Rewrite: Once you've written it down don't be frightened to change it if it doesn't say what you want.

5. Title:

Choose a title that's snappy, that summarises your testimony e.g. 'Free from Fear', 'I met Jesus', 'Don't pray for Me'.

6. Use:

Your tract won't make you an evangelist, but it will help you evangelise. Use it naturally on the bus or train as you chat to people. It's an aid – the Word of God won't return to Him empty.

WINNING CHILDREN TO CHRIST

In Matthew 18:1–14 Jesus challenged us about little children, how we should view and treat them, and the urgency of bringing them to Himself at an early and tender age.

Children have such a great advantage over adults in being able to receive Christ at an early age. Please, do not despise the decision of little children to invite Christ into their hearts. This decision is so valid in God's sight.

1.   Children are born humble

They grow proud as they get older. In fact they learn pride from adults. Jesus used a child in Matthew 18:2, 3 as a visual aid of humility. He did not say that the child should become as Peter or John, but instead, that they needed to become as the child, because children are good material for the kingdom. Someone once said that the door to the kingdom of heaven is only one metre high: adults have to bow low to enter, whereas children walk straight in.

2.   Children are teachable

They are at the key age of learning. They really want to know things. A child up to the age of seven has learned approximately half of all the knowledge they will know in life. They learn to crawl, walk, run, talk, use hands, feet, arms, feed themselves, read, and write, plus a whole lot more before that age. The capacity of a child to receive the Gospel is therefore tremendous.

3.   Children are curious

Their eyes are always open. They want to see what you are doing and hear what you are saying. Questions pour out incessantly from their lips: Why? When? How? They listen to anything you have to say about Jesus as long as you make it bright, cheerful and attractive.

4.   Children are used to receiving gifts

Gifts such as clothes, food, money, lollies, etc. Therefore it is not difficult for them to receive the gift of eternal life through Jesus Christ. However, adults feel that they have to work to earn the gift, seeing they have to work and sweat to earn a living.

5.   Children are dependent

They are conscious of need in their lives and look to older people to meet those needs. They are not too proud to ask. We adults think we are so independent, but we are not. We need God and we need each other.

6.   Children are greatly loved by Jesus

He said in Matthew 19:14 when the disciples had endeavoured to chase them away, 'Let the little children come to Me, and do not forbid them; for of such is the kingdom of heaven.' Children very easily see through a phony. They very soon tire of giving attention to someone who pretends to show an interest in them. They recognize genuine love and respond to it. I believe the little children flocked to the Lord Jesus. They loved Him because it was fun being with Him. He obviously did things that interested them and gave them the sense of security they needed. We need to be like Jesus to children if we are going to draw them to Christ in us.

7.   Children can believe on the Lord Jesus Christ

In Matthew 18:6, Jesus said, 'Whoever causes one of these little ones *who believe in Me* to sin, it would be better for him if a millstone were hung around his neck and he were drowned in the depth of the sea.' The words 'who believe in Me' indicate that children can have a very strong belief in the Lord Jesus Christ.

It has been said, 'If you reach an adult, you have salvaged only part of his life, but if you lead a child to Christ, you have saved a whole life.' One of the most precious testimonies is that of a child receiving Christ, growing up with a love and faith in the Lord Jesus that keeps them unscarred from the world's ravages.

Children and adults' outreaches

Reaching children and adults together

A child brought up in a Christian home can easily understand and respond to an adult message, but this is not the general rule. If children are present, rather gear the message to the children and their interests, adults will also understand and you'll reach the whole group together. Make sure the message is well illustrated verbally and visually.

Arrange children's Gospel activities alongside adult outreach functions

The enthusiasm of children can be used to bring non-Christian parents and older brothers and sisters to adult meetings.

Evangelistic outreaches specifically for children

The adult is shown his need of Christ by relating what the Bible says about things concerned with his everyday life – relationships, moral standards, emptiness, lack of direction, insecurity about the future.

A child's concerns are different – their world is simpler and smaller. They're still enjoying the excitement of new discovery and fantasy is still important to them, but they are aware of failure and the effect of sin in their lives.

The aim of children's outreaches

1.   To reap where seeds of the Gospel have been previously sown.

2.   To restore the interest of children who have become bored with the Gospel, by the stimulation of a different approach.

3.   To help in the maturing process of Christian children.

4.   To provide an opportunity for Christian children to invite and witness to non-Christian friends.

5.   To sow seeds in the lives of unchurched children.

6.   To bring them into a personal relationship with Christ.

Tips for reaching children effectively
The programme

Plan to use the best time of day, the best location, the age you desire to reach (it's very difficult to evangelise four year olds and fourteen year olds with the same approach). Use the gifts and talents of your helpers well, e.g. singing, drama, song leading, speaking, etc. Use as point of contact local events or interests that influence them. If you have boys and girls together, use illustrations concerning boys, you'll keep their attention and the girl's as well (tell a story about a girl and you'll lose the boys' attention).

Children's projects are very easy to organise. They do not have to be highly professional but they do need to be well organised and attractive to keep the children's attention. Your programme could include the singing of bright worship songs that are full of action, Bible games and quizzes that follow a particular theme, a key memory verse to establish a programme theme in their hearts, and then bright attractive drama, mime, puppetry, music, and sharing of testimonies using children to convey the reality of Christ in that child's life. It is always good to have a team work with you from your local church, to help with the organisation of the programme, its presentation, and especially the follow-up. In advertising your programme, use posters, handbills, radio, television, newspaper advertisements, or even a witness march using brightly coloured banners to attract the local children.

Should you be invited to speak to children's groups, such as primary schools, orphanages, and children's camps, etc. do not ever turn down those opportunities. Five or ten minutes is all you need to share the simple truths of the Gospel with them.

Use stories all the time to open up Biblical truths. Do this through colourful visual aids, such as flannel graphs, slides, films, or even the colourful plastic Good News Glove which Campus Crusade/Life Ministries distributes. I have used this little glove with great effect to win thousands of children to Christ in many parts of the world. Most Christian bookshops will have these marvellous visual aids available.

In fact, I have given Good News gloves to children I have trained in personal evangelism, so that they can use them as a point of contact to bring their friends to Christ. Let me tell you that children make the finest evangelists to children.

The 'King's kids' can put on 'Christian concerts' in which they present song items, dramas, clown skits and share their personal testimonies.

Wrap up the presentation with a very short Gospel message and then give an altar call.

Tips for communicating correctly with children

1. Spend an adequate time in prayer and in the Word of God. Stay in tune with Him.

2. In your attitude be loving and caring as you share with children. Many of their parents don't show much love and care. This will give you access into the children's hearts.

3. Be sincere and genuine as you share. Children see through a phony very quickly.

4. Be happy, excited and joyful as you share. A mournful, sad projection will lose their attention.

5. Don't talk down to them. Approach them on their level as their friend.

6. Research your subject matter well. There are many very good children's Bible story books available.

7. Use stories from the Bible, they are normally the best illustrations. Also use everyday up-to-date stories, obtainable from good Christian story books.

8. **(a)** Tell your story simply. A story is like a window letting light in for them to see the Gospel truth you are sharing. Keep the story short, so you come swiftly to your punch line.
    (b) Bring a Scriptural truth through the story.
    (c) Use a Bible verse or verses regularly through your Biblical truth to drive the point home. Don't use so many verses that you confuse them. Remember to keep it simple.
    (d) Use a couple of children from the audience as object lessons to illustrate your point. Never embarrass them, but encourage them.
    (e) Use visual aids freely, i.e. hand puppets, flannelgraphs, short dramas and plays and actions which you yourself can perform, cards with large key words on them can be a great help.
    (f) Use short films or slides to illustrate your theme.
    (g) Ask questions as you are sharing and encourage answers from the children.
    (h) Don't belittle them for their mistakes, even if they give a wrong answer rather say, 'You're getting close, see if you can give me something a bit closer to the answer'.
    (i) If they get restless, call firmly, but lovingly for their attention. You don't have to crack down hard on children.

(j)   Don't be loud and aggressive in speaking to children, use your normal tone of voice. If you are addressing a large crowd, rather use a public address system to project the sound.

When giving an altar call to children, keep it very short and unemotional. Children don't need begging and pleading to come to Christ. Simply ask them to bow their heads and pray a sincere prayer of commitment with you, emphasising that you are not forcing them to do it. They must only make this decision if they want to. You will find most of them will unashamedly pray aloud with you. Then simply ask those who prayed with you to stay behind while the others go, so that you can talk to them personally, and have counsellors chat with them. Of course, if this is the context of a public school or institution, arrange this with the authorities beforehand. If possible, don't leave the children at that point. Organise a series of *follow up meetings* with bright, attractive Bible studies to help them grow in Christ.

Counselling children

Counsellors should be made aware of the worth of a child; Jesus-appreciation of children; the need for children to be converted; how to make the child feel at ease; how to show them the need to receive Christ; how to lead them to Christ; and follow them up effectively.

Some important tips

– Keep your counselling sessions short.
– Avoid late night sessions, this will irritate parents.
– Don't put the children under pressure.
– Avoid making a decision too easy – they must realise the responsibility of being a disciple of Christ.
– Don't counsel behind closed doors – parents must have access to their children at all times.
– Avoid touching the child, they may react unfavourably, just shake their hand warmly.
– Counsel your own sex wherever possible.
– Use your Bible – if a child has one, show him verses in his Bible.
– Ascertain the nature of the decision, i.e. conversion, assurance, backsliding, a particular sin, a broken heart, a broken home situation, etc.
– Keep your counselling simple – don't confuse the child with unrelated doctrine.
– Use a well chosen verse of Scripture for each step of commitment:
– I am a sinner (Romans 3:23)
– I cannot save myself (John 6:47)
– Jesus loved me enough to die and take the judgement for my sin (John 3:16; Romans 5:8)
– I must be sorry and turn from the wrong things in my life (Acts 3:19)
– I must ask the Lord Jesus to forgive me and enter my life (1 John 1:9; Revelation 3:20).

Follow-up for children
(Especially when their parents have not made decisions for Christ)

1. Introduce the child to a small group of children within your fellowship where there is a loving, caring atmosphere providing teaching and fellowship.

2. Provide a friend who will bridge the gap between the child and the local church and will make friends with the child's parents.

Did you know that children can be most effective in reaching adults as well. Who can belittle the winsome efforts of a child who comes innocently to his father or some hardened relative and begins to share the love of Christ with her like, 'Don't you know, Granny, that Jesus loves you so much and died just for you ...?' As well as this, little children can trust God to heal the sick far more implicitly than adults can. Such innocent, expectant child-like faith is something we adults need to long for and treasure in ourselves. I am convinced that *God's giftings come not with maturity, but with humility*. Children have this humility and do not get swollen-headed when God uses them in the miraculous.

A life brought to Christ at a young, tender age can very easily be adjusted and redirected in the ways of God. However, when it reaches adulthood and maturity, the changes become so difficult to effect. The Lord Jesus still pleads today: 'Let the little children come to me and forbid them not!'

REACHING TEENAGERS WITH THE GOSPEL

Young people love to be ***dared and challenged*** to do things beyond the ordinary norms in their lives. They also love to have ***standards set*** for them – reasonable, attainable standards that cause them to rise above low standards of their peers. Very few do as they don't want to appear as a 'tall poppy' and have someone cut them down. However, in the heart of every young person is the desire to grow to full potential and be different. Young people hate to conform. This is why many do outrageous things to impress their peers, just to be different.

If you want to reach young people then challenge them, dare them to be different by committing their lives to Jesus Christ and rising up in the power of the Holy Spirit to be a powerful force for good in their community.

A great way to do this is ***not to focus on the negative*** in their lives ***but on the positive***.

That is the way God views you and me. That is the way He reviews our rebelling teenage population. He does not see them in terms of their rebellious attitude and outrageous acts. He sees them in terms of the tremendous potential and drive that they have for good. Sure the negative needs to be dealt with and disciplined, but do not focus on it. Focus on the positive, on what God can do with their lives by His grace if they will give themselves to Christ and follow Him. In Mark 1:16 and 17, Jesus said to His disciples, 'Come ye after me and I will make you to become fishers of men'. I believe what Jesus was saying was, 'If you put who you are and what you have in my hands, I will make you something related to what you were doing but so much more glorious and wonderful'. He has done that with our lives and He can do that with the most impossible of young people.

Young people are being dared by their friends into the drug scene and many horrific occult practices. Many are doing this simply because ***they are bored***. Others get involved because they ***do not want to conform to the hypocritical standards*** of the world that the adults have messed up. Challenge young people to ***dare to be different*** by committing their lives to follow Jesus Christ, the King of the universe, their interest is truly amazing.

Vital Factors to Communicate the Gospel to Teenagers

1.   They need to understand what the man Jesus was like in His humanity

He was a man's man in every sense – strong, rugged, as the carpenters of the day had to be. They had to cut down their own trees. Until the age of 30 Jesus Christ was a lumberjack as well as a carpenter. Can you imagine the muscular physique He had that commanded the respect of ***crude, rugged men of the world*** like Simon Peter, Andrew, James and John? When Jesus chased the money changers out of the temple they did not run from a weakling. When He swung the whip of cords above His head and His sleeves fell back, they saw the muscles this Man had and fled for their lives. *This is the MAN Jesus* – our Hero and a Man to be followed above all men. Challenge young people that He is the only one going in the right direction who is worth following and the only one who can change our lives by His mighty power. They do not have to be wimps in order to follow Christ. When they see the intellectual and social strength of the Man Jesus in the Gospels, they will be persuaded to follow in His footsteps. He desired to build spiritual strength in a person in order to make them a balanced and whole human being. This comes from standing close to Him in times of adversity, opposition and persecution. When young people are persuaded to take up this challenge they become men and women after God's own heart. They are able to show compassion to hurting humanity around them.

2. Young people need to be challenged not to be ashamed or frightened of Jesus

His great love caused Him to suffer and die, shedding His blood to forgive their sin and release them from a fruitless existence to live a powerful life in Christ. Share the events of the crucifixion with all its brutal detail, young people are moved to open their hearts to His wonderful love. I have seen crowds of young people moved to tears at the thought of a life so magnificent and beautiful being murdered so that His blood could be shed to rescue them from an empty meaningless life and a lost eternity.

3. Young people need a leader to follow ...

... and we must make them aware of who Jesus is. In Acts 10:36 He is referred to as the 'Lord of all creation'. John 1:3 tells us that nothing was made without Him. In Acts 3:15 He is referred to as 'the Lord of life'. When an egg and a sperm come together in a mother's womb, Jesus is the Author of that life. In 1 Corinthians 2:8 He is 'the Lord of Glory', which means in Heaven that Jesus is in charge. In Revelation 5:11 it says over a hundred million angels worship Him and are prepared to do His bidding. In Revelation 19:16 He is 'the King of kings and the Lord of lords'. To put it bluntly, Jesus is totally in charge. In the Greek the word for lord is 'kurios' which means Jesus is the Boss. When we let young people know, that as a Boss, Jesus is not a dictator or a tyrant but a loving, caring, providing Lord and Shepherd, it causes many who are tired and weary of life's struggles and burdens to yield their lives to Him. Then Jesus' marvellous promise in Matthew 11:28–30 can become a reality in their lives. Those who labour and are heavy laden can come to Him and find rest. Taking the responsibility of His Lordship and following Him upon their lives they find Him gentle and lowly in heart. They find following Him an absolute delight compared with the empty, frustrating burden of life without Him.

4. Share the power of the risen Christ with young people

The startling facts of the resurrection get their attention every time if shared in the right context. He was seen alive eleven times after His resurrection. He ate with His men twice and then at His ascension 500 saw Him visibly. These are proven historical facts, not just Biblical facts. Revealing this to young people challenges them to do something about facing up to the claims of the Lord who is alive and really can change them and their destinies.

5. They need to be introduced to the Holy Spirit and His awesome power

a) Share with them how the gifts of the Holy Spirit have operated through Words of Knowledge, Discerning of Spirits and the gifts of Healings resulting in wonderful healings and miracles.

b) Young people involved in witchcraft and occult practices have had the power of satan broken in their lives by the authority of the name of Jesus Christ. This results in many not only seeking help for their own deliverance but many committing themselves to follow the Lord Jesus. They have realised that it is far better to be on His side than on the enemy's side who is out to rob and kill and destroy their lives.

6. When leading young people to Christ ...

... challenge them straight away to make Him their King, Lord and Boss.

They are 'no nonsense' young people. They see through a phony immediately and do not want to be phonies themselves. When they can see in your life the true dynamics of a life yielded to the Lordship of Jesus, they will take up the challenge we are sharing with them. The youth of today are far tougher and more aggressive than the teenagers of yesteryear because present day times and circumstances have forced them to be so. A soft-sell Gospel message of a meek and mild Jesus no longer touches young people's hearts. *He is King and Lord. He is Master and Boss*. He is the *Leader in the column of progress* to our human destiny. *He is militant and strong against hypocrisy and unrighteousness* but so *tender and loving to those who know their need of Him*. Young people, deep in their hearts, want to able like this and will give their lives to follow this King and will sacrifice to the uttermost to help others to follow Him as well.

Invite questions from young people

Give them straight answers from the Word of God and your personal experience but be careful not to be distracted by irrelevant issues. Bring them back to the main issue at stake – that is their need to receive and follow Jesus Christ. If you do not know answers, do not waffle. Find the answers and get back to them. They will appreciate that far more than waffling. Do not be scared to talk about the *issues that really concern them today* such as:

• Political involvement

...but steer them along the lines of how to bring righteousness and peace into individuals lives that will eventually affect the nation. 1 Timothy 2:1–4 and Romans 13:1–7 give some direct answers in this area.

2. Sexuality

... do not be naive about the teenagers of the world today. In primary school they know what sexual intercourse is all about. They are asking a lot of questions so give them the answers from the Word of God from 1 Corinthians 6:9–20; Romans 1:18–27; Proverbs; 1 Thessalonians 4:1–8.

3. Pornography and blue films

... are a real issue with unchurched young people. God's Word speaks into this area in 1 Thessalonians 4:1–8 and James 1:13–16.

4. Community issues and unemployment

Let them know what the early church was doing in Acts 2:40–47 and 4:34–37. Many churches are functioning like that today.

5. They are very much against racism and sexism

... that the church seems to avoid speaking into. The Bible has some powerful answers in John 13:34 & 35, 17:20 & 21; 1 John 4:7–21; Matthew 5:43–48 and Ephesians 5:21–33.

6. They are appalled at the failings of the church

... with regard to a balanced ministry to the needy of the community. James 1:26 & 27 and James 2 show how some churches are getting it right.

7. The relevance of the Bible and prayer

... in one's daily life. Share with them from 2 Timothy 3:15 & 16; James 1:21; 1 Peter 2:2; Psalm 119:9 & 11; John 14:14 and Matthew 6:6–13 and they will realise that the Word of God and prayer has an awesome influence in a young person's life.

8. The results of a personal experience with God

God's Word has the answer in Matthew 6:33 and Matthew 7:7, Hebrews 2:6–11 and Hebrews 4:14–16.

Young people desperately want to know if there are solutions to these issues. God has been concerned enough to deal with them. The Bible has the answers. In caring for and following up young people who have come to Christ, *they have a tremendous desire for a 'father figure'* but in so many areas the Godly role of the father has disappeared and the young person has no role model to follow. We need to emphasise the nature and character of the Fatherhood of God.

Then there is the *desire for militancy and discipline*. We need to emphasise repentance and enlisting in the spiritual army of God for spiritual warfare against the forces of darkness in Christ's name.

They have an overwhelming *desire to be free from guilt and fear*. We need to preach the forgiveness of God and the cleansing and releasing power of the blood of Jesus Christ.

Finally they have a *desire to meet God and to know Him personally* not just know about Him. Encourage them with the fact that because Christ has redeemed them, forgiven and cleansed and clothed them with His righteousness they are 'accepted in the Beloved' and can definitely grow into an intimate relationship with God as Abba Father and they as His precious children.

Tips for communicating with teenagers

1. Spend an adequate time in prayer and in the Word of God to keep yourself in tune with the Holy Spirit.

2. Be prepared regarding the Scriptures, the subject matter of your message, illustrations and your method of approach, etc.

3. Be alert to the Holy Spirit to show you the needs in an individual's life. Ask the Holy Spirit and allow Him to operate His word of knowledge (revealing to you the needs) and His word of wisdom (giving you His solutions to those needs and problems). Don't point the person out publicly and embarrass them, invite those who are in need to see you privately afterwards.

4. As a point of contact use singers, song groups, short films, sporting heroes to share testimonies, but keep your supporting programme short. Remember your focal point is the call to a commitment and the counselling that follows. Everything else is aimed at that.

5. (a) Share stories from real life, such as dramatic events, heroism, etc.

(b) Use the Scripture directly. Have verses memorised and prepared relevant to your subject. Don't read them from the Scripture or read lengthy passages. Quote the verses and keep eye contact with your audience, otherwise you will lose their attention. As you have prepared, keep your thoughts in order and the points of your short message in line so as to avoid being distracted by noises, the looks on their faces, etc.

(c) Don't shout and scream. Keep your voice firm, clear and direct. Come from a position of strength, but in love.

(d) Be firm with disturbances in the group, call them to attention; they will respect your discipline. If you lose the antagonists as a result of the discipline, you'll certainly keep the attention of others. However, experience has proved that those you correct and discipline will give you attention as well.

(e) Be genuine and sincere. Let it show. In your talk use real life terminology, not Christian cliches that the non-Christians don't understand.

. Bring them to a personal decision for Christ. They may be embarrassed about making a public decision. Ask them to bow their heads and pray privately and quietly with you. You may invite them to come back to a follow-up session later in the day, or come and speak to you or a counsellor immediately or go through to an adjoining room to speak with a counsellor.

7.   Always be available afterwards for questions, counselling, etc. Let it be known that you are available. Remember that you are their point of contact at this point in time. They have warmed to your personality and approach.

8.   Leave good follow-up literature with them. Leave it in an accessible place where they can take it on the way out if they've made a commitment to Christ, or come and collect it from you or a counsellor.

9.   When counselling or talking personally with teenagers, don't speak down to them; don't judge them for their wrong way of life; let them know that you are their friend, especially by your attitude. Don't be condescending, remember you were once lost and mixed up as well. If they are seeking and wanting guidance, don't push them, offer them suggestions to the better way of life with Christ. If they are not ready to make a decision, don't push them, let them know they can call you for further help if they desire, you'll keep the door open that way. Then remember to pray constantly for them.

Involving and Training Christian Youth

Get young people involved with you. Equip them and they'll be the best point of contact to win young people to Christ. Here are opportunities to use young people:

1.   Train them how to reach their family and friends right where they are in everyday situations.

2.   Integrate young workers into your outreach and church programmes.

3.   Equip them to live the life of Christ in the market place of the world.

4.   Use young people's community projects as opportunities where young Christians can prove outstanding in service.

5.   Create youth task force teams to work in areas of social need, i.e. centres for the unemployed, orphans, old age homes, hospital projects, reformatories, etc.

YOU CAN WIN THE WOUNDED TO CHRIST

In Luke 9:10–17 we find the account of Jesus feeding the five thousand. Prior to this Jesus' men had been on a preaching tour and He presumably had been ministering for a time without their help. In order to take a break and rest up, Jesus and the disciples headed for a deserted place in order to get away from the crowd. However, the crowd noticed where He was going and followed Him. When they caught up with Him, He did not say, 'Oh no, not again. Give me a break. Can't you see we're tired? Besides that, it's after business hours. Come back on Monday'. There are three things that Jesus did in verse 11 that revealed His attitude to people. We have to have this same attitude and do what Jesus did if we are to win anyone to Christ, especially the heart-broken or those wounded in spirit.

In Luke 9:11 the Scripture says, '... He RECEIVED (welcomed) them, He SPOKE to them about the Kingdom of God, and He HEALED all those who had need of healing'. The psychiatrists tell us that one of the greatest causes of neurosis, nervous disorders, mental problems, loneliness and suicide is REJECTION – the feeling that we are not wanted; that people would rather have us go away, or that nobody cares.

A child is born into the love between its father and mother. If that love is soured the child feels rejected. It 'can't get in and snuggle down' – no security. As a result the child's heart is hurt and a rejection complex causes problems for the rest of its life. When we are born again, we are born into the love of the Trinity, between the Father, the Son and the Holy Spirit and we find ourselves very secure in that love.

When we are conceived God has a plan for our good and wellbeing as a result of His love! Satan tries to disrupt that plan with 'anti-love' – that is rejection.

Hurts that cause Rejection (tools of the devil)
At home
1. Wrong timing of a birth – too soon or too late in a marriage resulting in battered babies.

2. Wrong sex – a boy wanted instead of a girl or vice versa.

3. One child preferred by parents above another.

4. Parents always quarrelling or fighting – hurts taken in by the child.

5. Absent parent – dad in the army, parental desertion – the child loses its balance.

6. Parents too busy.

7. Separation from parents in hospital or given to a nanny for too long.

8. Cruelty instead of loving discipline.

9. Lack of loving cuddles.

At school

1. Teachers unkind.

2. Other children unkind.

3. Inability to cope with lessons – confidence undermined, parents too busy to help.

In courtship and marriage

1. Spouses unkind to each other.

2. Divorce.

In Church

Unwise and callous dealings by pastor or leadership.

Jesus never rejected anyone in need, even if it meant the sacrifice of His personal privacy. This is one of the most genuine sacrifices a person can be called to make.

In the process of winning the wounded we need to project the same attitude and really make them feel welcome and wanted. This is a prerequisite to fulfilling one of the most needed ministries in the world today and especially in the body of Christ.

When ministering to the wounded we must realise that *Jesus is the Healer of broken hearts but we have an important part to play* in the healing being effected. In John chapter 11 with the raising of Lazarus Jesus engaged His men as partners in asking them to remove the huge stone from the mouth of the tomb and then after He had raised Lazarus, told them to remove the bandages that bound his body. In the same way Jesus requires us to get alongside our hurting friends in order to care for them and 'roll away the stone of mistrust' and win their confidence. He requires us to really care for them and let His love and compassion flow through us to facilitate the healing that is needed. He then asks us to 'remove the bandages' that bind and hinder them. He requires us to counsel and deal with their fears and hurts that reveal themselves in symptoms such as:

(a) A tremendous insecurity and lack of confidence, where they are always saying 'I'm no good'.

(b) They have a 'no one wants me' attitude and for the most time are loners in life.

(c) They cannot accept love because they have never been given love. They cannot trust love because it has always come with a hurtful, ulterior motive.

(d) They bear anger and resentment and have a weird temper. Know that this is simply a defence barrier to protect themselves.

(e) They cannot accept criticism. It resonates through their hurts and they 'fly off the handle' very easily. They are extremely touchy people.

(f) They change jobs often. After settling down in employment, somebody is unkind or critical and they up and leave.

(g) On the other hand, some do things obsessively well to succeed in order to acquire recognition and acceptance.

The remedial action in dealing with a wounded soul is to:

1. Be a friend and show you really care

You are now in a prime position to imitate Jesus in the two remaining actions from Luke 9:11, i.e. speak to them about the Kingdom of God and heal those who have need of healing. We have the answers to all of mankind's needs and hurts in Jesus Christ. We do not have to offer poor excuses.

2. You will thus win their confidence and cause them to open up to you

When that happens listen to them. This is the key to being an excellent counsellor. As you listen to them (they will share all the symptoms) listen also to the Holy Spirit (He will show you the root cause). Let them know that Jesus really wants to heal them and set them free. Tell them according to Isaiah 53, He was 'despised and rejected of men', and knows what they are going through. Whilst He was being rejected by those He came to rescue He said, 'Father, forgive them they know not what they do'. This is the key to being healed of wounds caused by rejection.

3. The person you are endeavouring to win must forgive the one who has hurt them

Ephesians 4:32 is a key verse, 'Be kind and compassionate one to another, forgiving each other, just as in Christ, God forgave you'. If your friend is not a Christian this is a most marvellous opportunity to share the love of Christ and the purpose of His death upon the cross. When leading them to the Lord let them know that unless they forgive this will be a huge barrier hindering their relationship with God.

A backslidden Christian who has been wounded may be even harder to win back to the Lord because they may self-righteously want to justify bearing a grudge and refuse to forgive. Let them know that revenge is not sweet but will eventually poison every area of their life and destroy their relationships.

Encourage them to bring the one who has hurt them to God in prayer saying, 'Father I forgive them for what they have done to me. I release them into your hands'. Then they are in a position to ask God to forgive them for their bitterness, resentment and self-pity. Jesus taught us to pray, 'Forgive us our trespasses as we forgive them that trespass against us'. God cannot and will not forgive us while we bear unforgiveness toward others. This is an unconfessed sin and God cannot forgive sin unless it is confessed and dealt with in this manner. This is the only way that this seething wound is going to be healed.

If the person they have forgiven is constantly attacking them and the resentment creeps back they are to do what Jesus said in Matthew 5:44 and Luke 6:27 & 28, 'Love your enemies ... pray for those who persecute you ... bless them that despitefully use you'. An act of the will over the emotions is needed at a time like this. This will speed their healing process and ensure victory because they will find it very difficult to hate while they are praying in this manner.

4. If the 'hurt person' has been lured into a cult ...

...out of a need to find a refuge and belong where they are needed, they will need to be lovingly urged out of that destructive environment and surrounded with loving, caring people in your Christian community. I cannot over-emphasise the importance of a caring follow-up programme at this time which will ensure the person has every opportunity to be made whole and become fruitful in Christ.

5. Now apply the postive effect of the scriptures

Let them know from Ephesians 1:4–6 they are without blame before God in love and are accepted in the beloved. Let them know that their worth is not based on their acceptance or rejection by others but the fact that they are accepted by God. In terms of Colossians 3:3 they have died with Christ to sin and all its hurts and their life is hidden with Christ in God. In terms of Romans 8:31 & 37 if God be for them who can be against them, and they are more than conquerors through Christ who loves them.

Finally let them know from Matthew 12:20 that 'a bruised reed He will not break and a smoking flax (smouldering wick) He will not quench'. In old Israel the children would make little shepherd's whistles or flutes out of the bamboo reeds that grew at the river's edge. If a reed bent in the process it was useless for musical purposes and was thrown away. However, Jesus said a bruised reed of a human life He would not discard.

The Israeli homes of the day were lit by oil lamps in which floated a wick of flax. If the oil ran out during the night a terrible stench of smouldering flax would fill the house. The wick would have to be thrown away as it had no further use. Jesus said the smouldering wick of a broken life He would not put out. The King of Glory makes bruised reeds into beautiful instruments to play in His orchestra of grace and takes the smoking smouldering remnants of a human life and makes it into a bright light advertising His love and healing power to a hurting world. This is one of the greatest witnesses that a life reconstructed in Christ can have.

MINISTERING HEALING IN JESUS' NAME

1.   God desires you to be a whole person

God says in 3 John 2, 'Beloved I desire above all things that you should prosper (live in well-being) and be in health even as your soul prospers'. Therefore, as we prosper spiritually, the rest of our lives will experience God's abundance. God desires to meet all our needs, and has made provision for it in Christ's death and resurrection. Philippians 4:19, 'But my God shall supply ALL OUR NEEDS (salvation, healing, deliverance, release from a habit, financial needs, etc.) out of His vast riches in glory (in heaven and on this earth) through Christ Jesus'. 2 Corinthians 9:8, 'And God is able to make all grace (every undeserved heavenly favour and earthly blessing) ... *abound* towards you, so that you, always having an all sufficiency in all things, do have an abundance for every good work'. God's desire is plain. He desires us to experience His abundance and well being in every area and this includes healing for our bodies and minds.

2.   How God has made healing possible

Isaiah 53:3–5 '... a man of sorrows (pains) and acquainted with grief (sickness) ... surely He has borne our griefs and carried our sorrows ... and by His stripes (wounds) we are healed.'

1 Peter 2:24 '... ye *were* healed.'

Matthew 8:17 'He Himself took our infirmities and carried our diseases.'

He demonstrated God's healing power in His own ministry.

Matthew 4:23 'healing all manner of sickness and all manner of disease among the people.'

Acts 10:38 'God anointed Jesus with the Holy Spirit and with power and He went about doing good and healing all who were oppressed by the devil, for God was with Him.' The authority by which we can claim healing in any area of life is because Jesus bore every sickness, disease, weakness, and infirmity in His body through His wounds and stripes. If He bore them it does not make sense that we should bear them as well. We can be free. The *broken bread at the communion service* speaks of Christ's body given for us. His body was broken that our body may be made whole. Jesus said, 'This is my body which was given for you' – Luke 22:19.

3.   The method by which God enables us to heal is by the power of the Holy Spirit

Matthew 10:7–8 'As you go, preach saying the Kingdom of Heaven is at hand ... (you) ... heal the sick, raise the dead, cleanse the lepers, cast out devils. Freely you have received, therefore freely give.' Of what have we freely received in order to do this? THE POWER OF THE HOLY SPIRIT John 14:12 'Verily I say unto you, he that believeth on Me, the works that I do, shall he do also and greater works than these shall he do because I go unto My Father.' Jesus, after His mission was complete ascended back to the Father and sent forth the Holy Spirit to indwell us, to reign in our lives and to release His presence and power through us, SO THAT THE LIFE AND MINISTRY OF JESUS COULD BE DUPLICATED THROUGH EVERY SINGLE BELIEVER. Jesus said we *shall do* the works that He did. Let us therefore not let Him down but allow the Holy Spirit to operate through us performing the work of Jesus. The more people who grasp these facts the far wider the scale on which these works will be done.

4. The methods by which healing is imparted

Jesus said in Mark 16:17–18 'And these signs shall follow them that believe. In My name you shall cast out devils ... you shall lay hands on the sick and they shall recover.' The laying on of hands is simply a point of contact for the person to picture Jesus laying His hands upon them through you. You are operating under the authority of His name. Philippians 2:10 'At the name of Jesus every knee shall bow.' All sickness and disease, affliction and infirmity is subject to the authority of the name of Jesus. When you operate under the authority of His name, sicknesses and diseases are subject to you and your word, just as they were to Jesus and subsequently to His disciples. Mark 16:18, 'The sick shall recover.' Sometimes it happens instantly, sometimes progressively. It is operating under the authority of Jesus' name that releases the power of the Holy Spirit through you to minister to the needs of the needy.

5. Instructions in praying for the sick
James 5:14–16
(a) Call for the elders (responsible, God-anointed leaders) of the church who will anoint the person with oil in the name of the Lord and pray a prayer of faith over the one who is ill.

(b) The person must confess their faults to the person praying for them. A fault is not a sin, it is a weakness that trips a person into sin. If kept to one's self it becomes a monster lurking in the shadows, overwhelming the person, but when shared in confidence with the leader it is brought into the light and exposed for what it is. The leader prays for the person and the power of the fault is broken, no longer holding the person under its sway. (God says He will forgive any sin if we confess them *to Him*.)

6. How to deal with faults, barriers and prejudices

Always give the person time to think about any fault that may be present in their lives. These faults are barriers that hinder the person from confidently coming to God to have their needs met, as well as blocking God's power coming through to them. Here are some faults to mention to assist them: pride; doubt; fear; self-pity; seeking sympathy; wrong motives for wanting healing, i.e. not to glorify God but to follow their own lusts.

Unforgiveness is one of the largest single barriers that hinders a person's healing (including bitterness, resentment, hatred, bearing grudges, etc). They must:

(a) Forgive the person before God.

(b) Ask God's forgiveness.

(c) Go to the person and make right, if the person knows their attitude.

(d) Pray for the person that God will bless them. It will be very difficult to hate them and pray for them like that at the same time.

Involvement in the occult i.e. horoscopes, fortune-telling, the ouija board, attending seances, witchcraft, satanism, etc. This must be dealt with as follows (assuming the person is a Christian):

(a) They must confess this to God as a sin and ask forgiveness and cleansing in the blood of the Lord Jesus Christ.

(b) They must repent of their actions and renounce their association, cutting their ties with the occult involvement no matter how far in the past it has occurred.

(c) They must truly commit their lives to the Lord Jesus Christ and call upon His name for deliverance – Joel 2:32

(d) Only then does the leader pray for them in the following manner: Exercise the authority in the name of Jesus over the evil force by binding it, rebuking it and casting it away in the name of the Lord Jesus Christ, thus setting them free to receive from God.

7. The leader anoints them with oil in the name of the Lord Jesus

In Scripture, oil is the symbol of the Holy Spirit. It is a point of contact through which that person's faith is released to reach out to God for His supply of their need, and for the power of the Holy Spirit to begin flowing through them to perform their healing.

To aid you in praying for the person, picture in your mind the Holy Spirit healing them completely and see them by faith, free and healthy and well. A simple prayer to pray for the person is:

'I take the authority in the name of the Lord Jesus Christ over your infirmity. Because Jesus bore it in His body on the cross, by His stripes you are healed! Therefore I take the authority over your sickness in the name of the Lord Jesus Christ and I command it to go. I bless you in Jesus' name with life and strength and health. Amen.'

Spend a short time in praising the Lord and thanking Him for what He has done. Encourage the person to do so as well.

8.   What they should do following your prayer

They should go to someone and share the fact that they believe they have received healing on the basis that 'by Jesus' stripes they are healed.' This confession of faith establishes the fact in their hearts and lifts their faith to trust God further. They should thank the Lord as often as possible for their healing. This shows God their faith in advance of the result materialising. They should hold to the promises of God's Word, i.e. stand on God's promises regarding their healing. Give them verses such as: Isaiah 53:5; 1 Peter 2:24; Mark 16:17–18; James 5:14–15; Exodus 15:16 and Psalm 107:20; to hold onto and quote to the Lord in prayer daily regarding their healing, especially while they are waiting for the results to materialise in their body.

If they are on medication, tell them that unless the Lord shows them by a clear, specific revelation, they are *not to stop that medication*. The medicine will not stand in God's way of healing them and, in fact, God can very readily heal through medication and medical attention. It will be a very beautiful testimony unto the Lord for the doctor to give them a clean certificate of health. He will have to admit that God has performed a miracle. This will glorify God!

DELIVERANCE FROM SATANIC BONDAGE

Three Main Areas of Demonisation

Possession

– an evil spirit or spirits dwelling in a person's body controlling it at their will (e.g. the maniac of Gedara – Luke 8:26–39).

Obsession

– possession of the mind.

Oppression

– attacks by demonic spirits from without (depression etc.)

How do intelligent people get involved in this?

1. **Curiosity** – to know the future.

2. **Innocently** – to have a bit of 'fun', e.g. ouija board.

3. **Bereavement** – trying to contact a departed loved one through mediums and seances.

4. **Psychic experiences** – delving into the mystics for information and enlightenment.

5. **The Drug Scene** – drugs produce hallucinations through which satan and demons appear to the takers deluding them.

6. **The New Morality** – the sex orgies at satanic black masses and witches sabats give people licence to indulge their perverted sexual appetites.

7. **Communism** – spreading the occult practices in the West (although it is banned in Russia).

Satan's Subtle Trap

Like the Venus Fly Trap, it lures and destroys. Like a ladder, at the top, it starts with things that are seemingly 'innocent' and leads downward into the trap.

Horoscopes, astrology, fortune telling, tarot card reading, crystal ball gazing, palm reading, phrenology, teacup reading, handwriting analysis, clairvoyancy.

Yoga, Eastern cults, transcendental meditation, the martial arts – karate, judo, juijitsu, kungfu, etc.

Water divining, ESP, voodoo dolls, telepathy, hypnosis, pendulum-hypnosis, good luck charms and fetishes.

Ouija board, seances, spiritism, necromancy, spiritual or faith healing.

Witchcraft, satan worship, black masses, witches covens, sex orgies, human sacrifices.

Like a person starting out on the road to ADDICTION, one activity not satisfying the seeker leads on to the next and more involved activity; satan's object is to destroy God's creation.

God's Warning Against such Practices
Deuteronomy 18:10–12 exposes the following:
'Those that use divination' – fortune telling, ouija board, crystal ball, palmistry, phrenology, etc. to forecast the future.
'an observer of times' – an astrologer.
'an enchanter' – a person who deals in white or black magic; having weird, supernatural powers; a sorcerer.
'a witch' – a sorceress.
'a charmer' – a hypnotist.
'a consulter with familiar spirits' – a spiritist medium used by demon spirit guides at seances.
'a wizard' – a clairvoyant or psychic.
'a necromancer' – a medium who specialises in consulting 'the dead' to converse with them.
God calls these things and those who dabble in them an abomination.

Leviticus 19:31 exposes and warns against involvement in seances, clairvoyancy and psychic experiences.
Leviticus 20:6–7 God sets His face against those who consult familiar spirits at seances, and clairvoyants and psychics.
Galatians 5:19–21 God says those involved in idolatry and witchcraft will not inherit the Kingdom of God.
Isaiah 8:19 God says we are not to consult those who seek familiar spirits, clairvoyant and psychic experiences.
Exodus 22:18 God would not suffer a person involved in witchcraft or the occult to live.
Leviticus 20:27 Those involved in psychic experiences were to be stoned to death.
Other verses: Isaiah 47:12–13; 2 Kings 23:24; Micah 5:12; Luke 11:24–26; Acts 19:19; Revelation 9:21, 21:8, 22:15.

God's anger is invoked because of occult involvement:
1.   It is open disobedience to God's Word and an abomination to Him.

2.   Breaks the first commandment and invokes God's curse – Exodus 20:3–5.

3.   Rejection of God's revealed will through His Word and rejection of fellowship with Him.

How do evil spirits gain access?

1. Indulging in occult practices.

2. Wilfully practising sin (fornication, resulting in sexual perversion).

3. Emotional crises (shock, prolonged grief, fear, etc).

4. Doubt, scepticism or constant ridiculing of divine things (this results in constant unbelief and rejection of God's Word which is rebellion against God which could open the door to force of evil).

5. Unforgiveness one toward another, prolonged bitterness and resentment. It opens the door to demon forces resulting in oppression and depression.

Symptoms shown by someone bound by demonic forces

1. **Possession:** uncontrollable temper and hatred; afflicting one's own body; lingering sickness and diseases that doctors are unable to cure (a spirit of infirmity); certain manifestations, e.g. weird screams, devilish laughter, weeping, ravings, uncontrollable cursing; frothing at the mouth; personality changes; sexual abuse and perversion; certain addictions which are not brought under control and conquered.

2. **Obsession:** uncontrollable intense fear; chronic, constant unbelief (demons can prevent a person from believing scriptural truths if the Word is constantly rejected); uncontrollable lying and anger; insane jealousy; uncontrollable envy; resentment; lust; strife; pride; unforgiveness; seduction; torment or restlessness.

3. **Oppression:** depression; despair; disappointment that will not go; constant discouragement which leads to suicide; chronic headaches; e.g. migraine that resists medical treatment.

Recognise that depression and other attacks from without are called by Scripture, a 'spirit of heaviness' – Isaiah 61:3.

The remedy – Joel 2:32 'Call on the name of the Lord = deliverance'.

To keep one's deliverance from depression – Isaiah 61:3 says, 'wear the garment of praise'.

Some sound advice

1. Don't go round looking for a demon in every problem (they may just need counselling in an area not yielded to the Lord), but be prepared for action when required.

2. In the absence of obvious symptoms rely on the Holy Spirit to operate 'the gift of discerning of spirits' through you.

3.   Don't start casting a demon out of someone unless you are sure of its presence. Ask someone who has had experience in this field to help you.

4.   If you do start casting out a demon when one is not present, you could cause all sorts of mental and psychological problems.

How to deal with someone bound by satanic forces
When can help be given?
1.   When they want help.

2.   When the power of God is released in the situation.

3.   When they are unconscious.

REALISE THAT YOU HAVE POWER AND AUTHORITY OVER SATAN AND EVIL FORCES IN THE NAME OF THE LORD JESUS CHRIST!

Demons have respect for the power of the Holy Spirit and the authority of Jesus Christ in which you move and operate. When you use the name of Jesus and operate under its authority, you have all the power that Heaven can muster behind you – Luke 10:19 'Behold I give you power ... over all the power of the enemy and nothing shall by any means harm you.' Mark 16:17 'These signs shall follow them that believe ... in My name they shall cast out devils ...' Matthew 10:7–8 'Cast out devils ...' Don't be frivolous in these dealings but don't be afraid. You take the authority over the evil forces and command them to go, releasing their hold on the person IN JESUS' NAME.

If you're not sure of the person's condition, i.e. whether a demon is present or not, or whether it has left the person, test the spirits – 1 John 4:1–3. They will never admit that Jesus Christ is come in the flesh and is Lord. They will answer in the negative.

How to pray with a person for deliverance
1.   If they are a Christian already, but backslidden or having dabbled in the occult, get them to re-affirm their faith in Christ and re-dedicate their life to the Lord. If they are not born-again Christians, lead them to Christ first.

2.   They must confess their backsliding or occult involvement to God as a specific sin and ask cleansing in the blood of Jesus. They must then thank Him for it – 1 John 1:9. They must do this aloud in your presence.

3.   They must renounce all association and cut all ties with their occult practices.

4.   They must command satan and the evil forces to depart from their lives – James 4:7.

5.   They must then ask God for deliverance from their bondage – Joel 2:32.

6.   Then you pray for them, taking the authority over the satanic, demonic forces in the name of Jesus Christ, breaking their power and influence and commanding them to leave the person once and for all.

Acts 10:38 describes Jesus' ministry. John 14:12 was Jesus' teaching that we should continue His ministry in the power of the Holy Spirit upon this earth, and this includes leading people through to deliverance.

How to lead a victorious Christian life and keep one's deliverance

1. Revelation 12:11 'And they overcame the devil by the blood of the Lamb, and by the Word of their testimony ...' They must know their authority and position through the blood of Jesus Christ which redeems them out of satan's hand, and use it in their testimony against the devil. The devil is a defeated enemy. Christ's death on the cross stripped him of his power and authority. Those who believe in Christ enter into His victory over the devil. So the outcome of our battle with these powers of darkness is never in question. Our ground of victory through the blood is adequate and sure.

2. Be constantly filled with the Holy Spirit and walk in the Spirit, not after the lusts of the flesh.

3. Stay away from occult practices.

4. Keep the 'old nature of sin' crucified (Galatians 2:20).

5. Wear the garment of Praise (Isaiah 61:3).

6. Fellowship with other Christians regularly (1 John 1:7).

7. Cut the association with those who would draw you back into sinful or occult activities (2 Thessalonians 3:6; 1 Corinthians 5:9; Ephesians 5:11).

8. Act against what satan tries to get you to do; reject his influence (James 4:7).

9. Wear the 'whole armour of God' – Ephesians 6:10–17. All these items of armour refer to the Lord Jesus: – Romans 13:14 'Put on the Lord Jesus Christ'.
Ephesians 6:14 **'Loins girt with truth'** – Jesus is the TRUTH dwelling in us inspiring us to live truthful lives (John 14:6).
:14 'Breastplate of righteousness' – He is our righteousness, which inspires us to righteous living (2 Corinthians 5:21).
:15 'Feet shod with the Gospel of Peace' – He is the Prince of Peace and it's His Gospel we carry (Isaiah 9:6).
:16 'Shield of Faith' – He is the Author and Finisher of our faith (Hebrews 12:2).
:17 'Helmet of Salvation' – He is the Captain of our Salvation – (Hebrews 2:10).
:17 'Sword of the Spirit' – The Word of God – Jesus is the Living Word, made manifest through the written Word which when we quote into a situation is a 'sharp two-edged sword' out of our mouths (Hebrews 4:12; John 1:18).

SIMPLY ABIDE IN CHRIST: STAY CLOSE TO HIM AT ALL TIMES.

THE FULNESS OF THE HOLY SPIRIT

Three questions ...

1. Does the Holy Spirit Reside in You?

If you have truly believed in the Lord Jesus Christ and received His offer of forgiveness, salvation and eternal life, the answer is YES. 1 Corinthians 12:13 'For by one Spirit we were all baptised into one body ... and we were all made to drink of one Spirit.' This happens at salvation. When we receive Jesus He comes to live in us in the person of the Holy Spirit and He moulds the image of Christ in us. He gives us the nature of Christ thus we become a new creation in Christ Jesus. Jesus in bodily form is seated at the right hand of the Father in heaven interceding for us. So it is a physical impossibility for Jesus Himself to live within us. He lives in us by the Holy Spirit who makes Jesus real to us. Romans 8:9 'But if anyone does not have the Spirit of Christ, he does not belong to Him.'

2. Does the Holy Spirit Reign in You?

2 Corinthians 3:17 'Now the Lord is that Spirit and where the Spirit of the Lord is (where the spirit is LORD) there is liberty'.

Where the Holy Spirit reigns in our lives, not just resides, but reigns, we have liberty. It is not enough to say 'Lord I give you my life'. We must give the different aspects of our lives particularly the problem areas, over to the Holy Spirit to reign and exercise His Lordship over those areas. Remember, He is the personality of the Godhead upon this earth at this point in time, therefore He is God, co-equal with the Father and Son, Jesus Christ. When the Holy Spirit is not in control of an area of our lives we do not have liberty in that area, and therefore experience an element of bondage.

The Holy Spirit so much desires to rule in every area of our lives, such as:

(a) The 'first impression' area that is seen by people. Our motives must be to draw them to Christ, not impress them with our personal virtues.

(b) The area of recreation, pleasure and entertainment.

(c) Our plans, aims and ambitions for the future.

(d) The books we read, the movies we see, the things we feed our mind on.

(e) Our secret lives, which includes the sexual area of our lives.

(f) The inner closet of our lives – where so often we have the image of self, ego and pride enthroned. The Holy Spirit desires that we should get off that throne and allow Him to enthrone the Lord Jesus Christ.

The Holy Spirit desires to 'control' our lives; not as robots or puppets, but as men and women of courage and character, yielded to Him, under His influence and to obey Him and follow His guidance.

Galatians 5:22–23 'But when the Holy Spirit controls our lives, He will produce this fruit in us: love, joy, peace, patience, kindness, goodness, faithfulness, gentleness and self-control ...' The mark of spirituality is not the number of gifts operating in a person's life, but the evidence of the fruit of the Holy Spirit.

This applies to a church or fellowship as well. Jesus said, 'By this shall all men know that you are my disciples if you have love one to another.' (John 13:35)

The essence of the Spirit-filled life is not 'how much of the Holy Spirit do I have?', because we have all of Him, but 'how much of us does He have?' It does not only mean to be 'filled up' with the Holy Spirit, but to be yielded to and living under his influence/control.

Ephesians 5:18 'And do not get drunk with wine (be under the influence of liquor) ... but be filled with (be under the influence of) the Holy Spirit.'

3.   Has the Holy Spirit been Released Within You?

John 7:37–39 – Jesus said, 'If anyone is thirsty, let him come to me and drink. He who believes in Me as the Scripture said, from his innermost being shall flow rivers of living water. But this spake He of the Holy Spirit whom those who believe in Him would receive.' Acts 1:4–5 – 'And gathering them together Jesus commanded them not to leave Jerusalem but to wait for what the Father promised, "which you heard from Me, for John baptised with water, but you shall be baptised with the Holy Spirit, not many days from now".'

Acts 1:8 – Jesus said, 'But you shall receive power when the Holy Spirit has come upon you, you shall be my witnesses ...' Acts 2:1–21, 37–39 describes the outpouring of the Holy Spirit upon the early disciples. They were filled with, baptised with, drenched with the presence and power of the Holy Spirit. Jesus desires to do the same with us. He desires to release the presence of the Holy Spirit from within us to fill us and overflow from our lives; drenching us and immersing us in His presence and power. The reason for which the Lord Jesus baptises us in the Holy Spirit is to give us *power, boldness and confidence to witness* and share our faith in Jesus with others. This experience changed the early disciples from cowards into bold, courageous people who were even prepared to sacrifice their lives for Jesus and the Gospel.

I have learned that I must come to the Lord regularly for a re-filling of the Holy Spirit's power. Scripture says that we are to be continually filled with the Holy Spirit. We need to wait on Him in prayer each day to fill us afresh and drench us with His presence and power. This we need for a continuing ministry of outreach and evangelism. The main reason for which the Lord blesses us with the fulness of the Holy Spirit is to reach others. Acts 1:8 – 'You shall be My witnesses'. Many who have been baptised in the Holy Spirit are today relatively powerless because they have not sought the power of the Lord continually for re-filling after re-filling in the Holy Spirit. They may even be able to speak in tongues and operate other gifts of the Holy Spirit, but the power of the Holy Spirit has 'leaked out' through the cracks in the vessel of their lives, i.e. sin, disobedience, grieving the Holy

Spirit, resisting Him. When someone says 'I am filled with the Holy Spirit' God desires to see the power of the Holy Spirit flowing through their lives, resulting in a powerful, personal witness that brings people to Christ.

Two Qualifications for the Baptism in the Holy Spirit

1. You must be a child of God, having received the Lord Jesus Christ as your Lord and Saviour.

2. You must desire the baptism in the Holy Spirit. God will not force anything on someone who does not want it.

How do you receive the Baptism in the Holy Spirit?

Simply ask in faith. Luke 11:9–13 – 'Ask and you shall receive ... if you then being worldly know how to give good gifts to your children, how much more shall your Heavenly Father give the Holy Spirit (in all His fulness) to them who ask'.

Jesus's method for the Baptism in the Holy Spirit

1. 'If any man is thirsty ...' We must earnestly desire the baptism in the Holy Spirit.

2. 'Let Him come to Me' – we came to Him for salvation, now we come to Him as the Baptiser in the Holy Spirit.

3. '... and drink ...' We must draw from Him in prayer, i.e. we must breathe this in and 'drink' from the fountainhead of the Lord.

4. 'He that believeth on Me ...' We believed on him for salvation, now we must believe by faith that He is filling us the moment that we ask. Don't let your reason interfere and shut off the flow of the Holy Spirit that has begun in you.

5. 'Out of your innermost being shall flow forth rivers of living water.'

This begins to happen; whether we feel it or not, the moment we ask, if we have fulfilled the Lord's simple conditions.

The normal attestation that a person has been baptised in the Holy Spirit or received the fulness of the Holy Spirit is that they are given a *new prayer language* which the Bible calls 'speaking in other tongues'. This the disciples experienced in Acts chapter 2 and were given as a Spirit-aided means of prayer and praise unto our Heavenly Father. This is the gateway into the operation of the gifts of the Holy Spirit. He operates these gifts through a Spirit-filled believer, therefore all these nine gifts are inherent in the Spirit-filled believer, for the Holy Spirit to operate at any time. It is our responsibility to be sensitive to His moving to be used by Him in the area of these gifts. (The word 'gifts' means a gifting or an enduement for the specific avenue of service.)

If a person does not speak in tongues immediately, they must not be discouraged. The Lord has nevertheless begun to fill them and will bring it to fruition. *The evidence that they are filled is the power of their witness.* Encourage them to seek the Lord for the utterance in tongues, knowing the wonderful benefits of this gift. It edifies, uplifts and strengthens the believer as he communicates with the Lord in other tongues.

Two barriers that hinder many from coming into the Baptism in the Holy Spirit

1. Unforgiveness one toward another. This needs to be dealt with by:
   (a) Forgiving the person before God.
   (b) Asking God's forgiveness themselves.
   (c) Going to that person and making things right.

2. Dabbling in the occult. This must be dealt with in accordance with the notes on deliverance.

As a counsellor leading someone into the Baptism in the Holy Spirit, after giving them this simple instruction, pray with them as follows:

1. Let them ask the Lord Jesus personally, out loud, to fill them and baptise them in the Holy Spirit.

2. Then they lift their heads up, open their mouths and begin to 'drink', i.e. breathe in the presence of the Lord. This is simply a point of contact to open themselves up to the baptism in the Holy Spirit.

3. If they are tense and rigid, get them to *praise the Lord* out loud for who He is and His goodness toward them.

4. Help them to realise that the Lord has certainly begun to fill them from the moment they asked.

5. Encourage them to speak out in other tongues if it wells up in them or the Holy Spirit puts the words into their minds. They are the ones who must do the 'speaking'. The Holy Spirit will not grab their tongue and shake it.

6. As their counsellor keep very much in tune with the Holy Spirit for the *interpretation of that 'tongue'* or language they utter. It will be a great encouragement to them to know that they are actually praising God in another language. In every instance when a person speaks in other tongues it is either a prayer or a praise unto God. Acts 2:11 '. . . we hear them in our own language speaking of the mighty deeds of God'.

7. If they do speak in tongues, encourage them to *exercise that gift* in their personal devotional life and praise the Lord all the more in that way. Encourage them not to let the devil cause doubt in their minds regarding this. It is definitely from the Holy Spirit, not them making it up. If they have not spoken in other tongues, encourage them to continue seeking the Lord for this utterance and then